SUNRISE OVER STONE PINES IN THE COTO DOÑANA, SPAIN

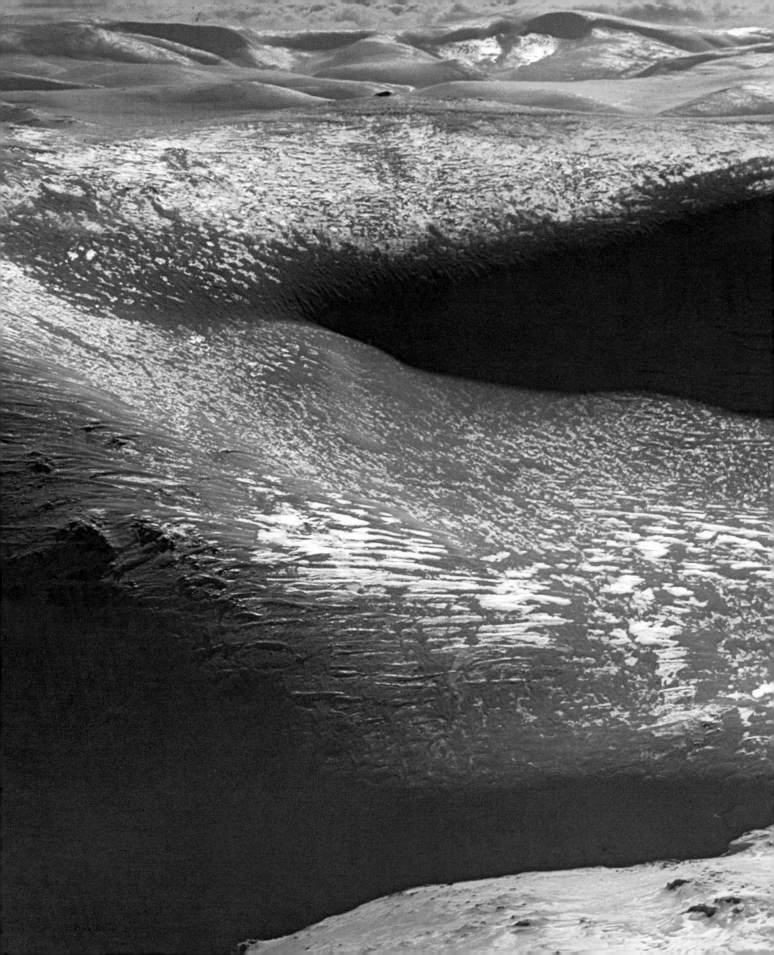

WINTER IN THE CAIRNGORM MOUNTAINS, SCOTLAND

EUROPEAN EDIBLE FROGS CROWD A SWISS POND

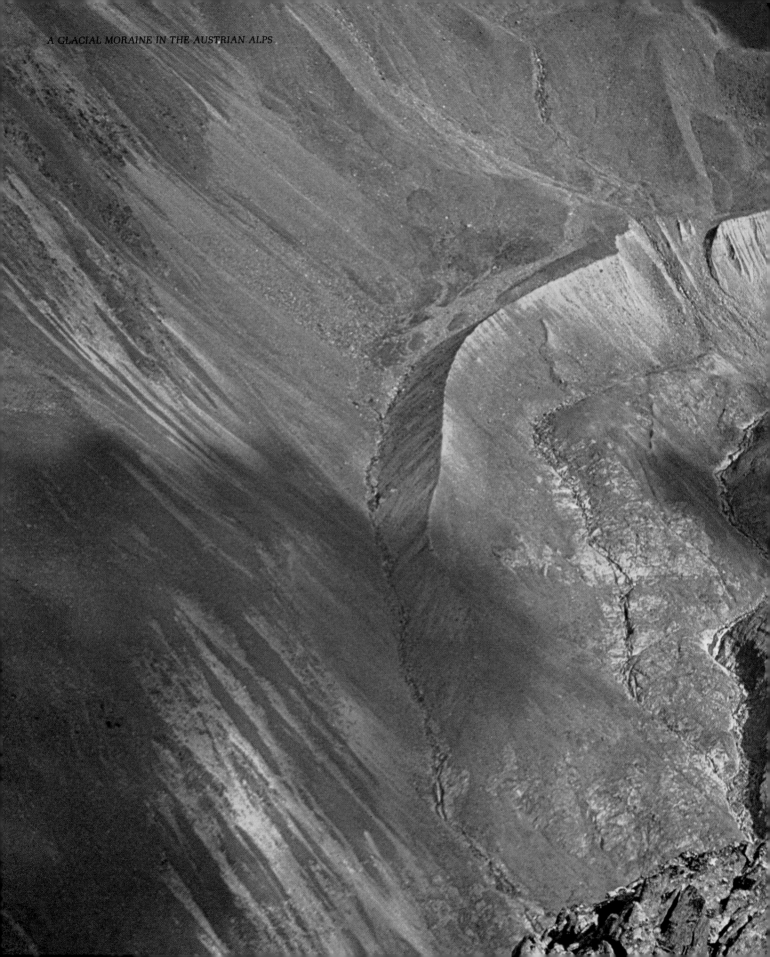

WILDERNESS EUROPE

THE WORLD'S WILD PLACES/TIME-LIFE BOOKS/AMSTERDAM

BY DOUGLAS BOTTING
AND THE EDITORS OF TIME-LIFE BOOKS

*For the first time in Earth's history, our species has the capacity
to violate the environment on a scale that endangers the
existence of all species. The heedless exploitation of nature
and the careless use of resources already threaten our
inheritors with a world physically and spiritually impoverished.*

DECLARATION OF THE 14TH BIENNIAL WILDERNESS CONFERENCE, PRESENTED TO THE U.N., 1975

THE WORLD'S WILD PLACES

European Editor: Dale Brown
Editorial Staff for *Wilderness Europe:*
Deputy Editors: Christopher Farman, Simon Rigge
Picture Editor: Pamela Marke
Design Consultant: Louis Klein
Staff Writers:
Michael Brown, Norman Kolpas,
Heather Sherlock, Deborah Thompson
Text Researcher: Vanessa Kramer
Art Director: Graham Davis
Designer: Joyce Mason
Picture Researchers: Karin Pearce, Susan Stratton
Picture Assistants: Cathy Doxat-Pratt, Thelma Gilbert,
Christine Hinze, Marilyn Miller
Editorial Assistants: Ellen Brush,
Elizabeth Loving, Jackie Matthews
Copy Staff: Jan Piggott, Julia West
Revisions Staff:
Researcher: Nicola Blount
Sub-Editor: Frances Dixon

Consultants
Botany: Christopher Grey-Wilson, Phyllis Edwards
Geology: Dr. Peter Stubbs
Herpetology: David Ball
Icthyology: Alwyne Wheeler
Invertebrates: Michael Tweedie
Ornithology: Dan Freeman
Zoology: Dr. P. J. K. Burton

The captions and text of the picture essays were
written by the staff of Time-Life Books.

ISBN 7054 0159 6

TIME-LIFE is a trademark of Time Incorporated U.S.A.

Published by Time-Life Books B.V.
Ottho Heldringstraat 5. 1066 AZ Amsterdam.

The Author: Douglas Botting, London-born and Oxford-educated, is a writer and photographer who has been on many scientific and film expeditions to wild places around the world. He has travelled to Arctic Siberia and to southern Arabia, across East Africa in a balloon and down the River Orinoco in a hovercraft. He was a member of the Mato Grosso Expedition organized by the Royal Society and by the Royal Geographical Society, of which he is a Fellow. He has made many documentary films for television and is the author of several books on history and travel, including a biography of the German explorer and scientist, Alexander von Humboldt.

The Consultant: John Burton, Executive Secretary of the Fauna and Flora Preservation Society, is a naturalist and zoogeographer with an extensive knowledge of European wild places and a strong interest in conserving the continent's remaining wildlife. He is the author of several books on wildlife and co-author of the Collins *Field Guide to Amphibians and Reptiles of Europe.* In *Wilderness Europe* he wrote the nature walk, about a trip with Douglas Botting through the Danube Delta.

The Cover:
A blanket of honey mushrooms and nettles covers the entire 100-foot trunk of a wind-toppled hornbeam tree in the primeval Bialowiecza Forest on the Polish–Soviet border. Bialowiecza, with its giant oaks, limes and hornbeams, its pines and spruces, is one of the few surviving remnants of the mixed forests that covered much of Europe before the emergence of agricultural man.

Contents

MILES

0 100 200 300 400

N

Norwegian Sea

The Faeroes

Shetland Islands

Page 160

Orkney Islands

Hebrides

Caledonian Mountains

Continental Shelf

North Sea

Lofoten Islands

Caledonian Mountains

Jostedal Ice Cap

NORWAY

OSLO

SWEDEN

Gulf of Bothnia

FINLAND

HELSINKI

STOCKHOLM

Gotland

Öland

Baltic Sea

DENMARK

COPENHAGEN

River Shannon

DUBLIN

IRISH REPUBLIC

UNITED KINGDOM

AMSTERDAM

NETHERLANDS

HARZ MOUNTAINS

EAST BERLIN GERMANY

POLAND

Masurian Lakes

Biebrzanskie Marshes

River Vistula

BIALOWIESKI PARK NARODOWY

Marshe

WARSAW

Pripet

LONDON

BRUSSELS

BELGIUM

River Rhine

BONN

M

LUXEMBOURG

WEST GERMANY

PRAGUE

River Vltava

CZECHOSLOVAKIA

Lysa Gora Plateau

u

t

a

i

n

s

TATRA MOUNTAINS

C
A
R
P
A

Atlantic

Ocean

PARIS

FRANCE

Black Forest

VOSGES

R
h
i
n
e

BERNE

SWITZERLAND

P

S

AUSTRIA

VIENNA

Neusiedlersee

Hungarian Puszta

BUDAPEST

HUNGARY

ROMAN

Bay of

Biscay

Rhône

Page 49

PARC NATIONAL DE HAUTE-SAVOIE

Mont Blanc 15,78 ft.

L

DOLOMITES

PARCO NAZIONALE GRAN PARADISO

River Po

Po Delta

Lake Kisbalaton

BUCHAR

Camargue

MASSIF CENTRAL

R
i
v
e
r

A

PARCO NATIONALE DE LA VANOISE

NICE

CANNES

ITALY

BELGRADE

YUGOSLAVIA

Adriatic

SIERRA DE CANTABRIA

River Douro

P Y R E N E E S

C

H

PARCO NAZIONALE DEGLI ABRUZZI

Sea

PORTUGAL

MADRID

SPAIN

Corsica

A
P
P
E
N
N
I
N
E
S

ROME

Vesuvius

GREECE

PARNASS

LISBON

Balearic Islands

Sardinia

Tyrrhenian Sea

CALABRIA

Stromboli

Ionian Sea

ATHEN

SEVILLE

Page 110

River Guadalquivir

Las Marismas

SIERRA NEVADA

TABERNAS

Lipari Islands

MESSINA

PARQUE NACIONAL DEL COTO DE DONANA

ALMERIA

Cabo de Gata

Etna

Sicily

Mediterranean

Sea

GIBRALTAR

Gozo

Malta

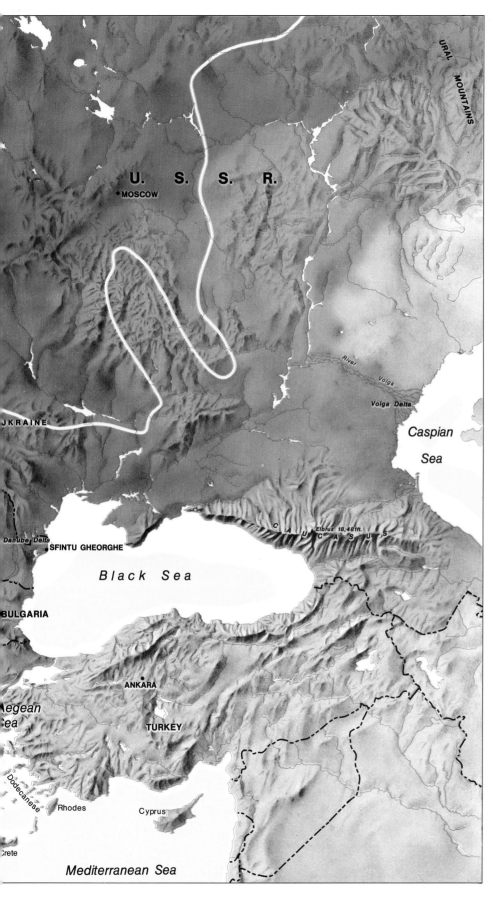

The Natural Features of the Continent

The sprawling continent of Europe, with its peninsulas and islands, includes all the land area on the map except those parts coloured grey. Most of the landscape has been modified by man, but the underlying features remain dictated by the unchallengeable forces of geology and climate.

Great mountain ranges mark the zones where the continent's crust has crumpled under tectonic pressures: in the north-west are the ancient Caledonian mountains; in the east, the Urals form the natural divide between Europe and Asia; in the south lie the vast curve of the eroded Hercynian mountains and the sharp-ridged mass of the young Alpine ranges.

During the last great Ice Age, which ended 10,000 years ago, ice sheets covered much of Europe, and the Atlantic coast lay as far west as the edge of the continental shelf. When the climate became warmer, the seas rose to give Europe its familiar outline, the ice retreated to its present smallholdings, and four broad vegetation zones were spread across the continent (all except the far northern tundra are illustrated on the map). Of the natural vegetation that dominated these zones, only a few remnants have escaped destruction by man, and they survive, in the main, as nature preserves. They are among Europe's last wild places.

On the map, the coniferous zone is grey-green; the deciduous zone, green; the Mediterranean zone, pale green. Permanent ice cover is white, and the maximum extent of Ice Age glaciation is marked by white lines. Sea down to 600 feet is white; deeper than that it is blue. Nature preserves discussed in the book are marked in red. Boxed areas are enlarged on the pages indicated.

1/The Last Wild Places

---

*I am convinced that man has suffered in his separation from
the soil and from the other living creatures of the world;
the evolution of his intellect has outrun his needs as an
animal, and as yet he must still, for security, look long at
some portion of the earth as it was before he tampered with it.*

GAVIN MAXWELL/*RING OF BRIGHT WATER*

All afternoon the barometer had been falling and by dusk the needle had
dipped to "Stormy". The sea in the small bay in front of the house was
still smooth, but the clouds were beginning to stream and I knew that before long it was going to blow. The weather forecast only confirmed what
I knew. "Attention all shipping!" the radio said. "Here is a gale warning.
Iceland, Faeroes, Rockall, Hebrides. Strong to gale force winds, north-
west backing westerly Force 9, rising to whole gale Force 10, imminent."

The old lighthouse keeper's cottage in which I was wintering on the
West Highland coast of Scotland lay in the path of the coming storm.
From the door of the cottage, only a stone's throw from the shore, I could
look straight out to sea, and between me and Hudson Bay and the Labra-
dor coast of North America lay nothing but a few small islands and 2,500
miles of the wild North Atlantic. Only the tall Hebridean Isle of Eigg 20
miles away, in profile like the statue of a recumbent lion, gave some
slight protection from the furious winter winds that swept across the
Western Approaches and fell violently upon the Highland coast. In the
gathering gloom I dragged the dinghy up the beach beyond the spring
tide line, and turned it over and lashed it down. Anything that could be
blown away I put inside the house, and I fastened the doors and windows
securely. Then, like an old sea salt in mid-ocean, sails reefed and hatches
battened down, I waited for the storm to do its worst.

The cottage was built on a broad patch of sandy turf and marram grass beside a bay near the Sound of Sleat, opposite the Isle of Skye. It had the sea to the front of it, a waterfall and a swift-flowing burn at the back of it, and a hillside of bracken and conifers to one side, rising steeply to the snow-covered summit of Ben Sgreol 3,200 feet above. No light-house keeper had lived there for years, for the lighthouse on one of the near-by islands was automatic, and the place was now the Highland retreat of a friend of mine—the writer and naturalist, Gavin Maxwell. He had written a book about his life there and the otters that shared it with him, a book that became a classic of its kind, called *Ring of Bright Water*. To the few square miles of natural paradise which were its subject he gave the name Camusfearna, which is Gaelic for Bay of Alders— a name that cannot be found on any map.

One winter when his work required his absence abroad, Gavin asked me if I would act as locum and look after the otters until his return. I had recently returned from the Sahara, intending to write a book myself, and Camusfearna seemed an ideal place in which to do it, or so I believed at the time. Late in October, therefore, when the geese in long arrow-head skeins were passing high overhead on their way to winter quarters in the south, I arrived at Camusfearna. It was to be May before I saw shops or traffic again, or human faces in groups greater than two.

I had always been drawn to wild places, to the virgin wilderness and the frontier country, and a large part of my adult life had been spent in the remoter corners of Africa, Asia and South America. I had never believed a wild Europe existed. It was, I felt, a contradiction in terms. I had been born in London a few steps from one of the lesser tributaries of the Thames, a stream called Beverley Brook. It had once been a beaver stream, but the beavers had long since gone and Beverley Brook was representative of its type all over modern Europe: hunted out, built over, tamed. So Camusfearna that winter was a shock: for the first time I was confronted with the reality of a wilderness in my own continent.

It was sometimes difficult to believe that a place so wild and isolated could still exist in a country as densely populated as Britain. If gales lifted off the roof of the cottage, or if I fell and broke a leg, there would be no easy way to summon help. There was no telephone, no way in or out by sea in bad weather. The nearest road was three miles away, over the trackless peat bogs. The nearest human settlement was some miles down that road. Otherwise Camusfearna was the haunt of dolphins and shearwaters in a world of rock, moor and water.

Living there was like living at a polar station. The pale northern sun climbed less and less each day and before long it was so low at noon that my body cast a shadow almost 50 feet long. The snow line crept lower and lower down the flanks of Ben Sgreol. My provisions came by mail boat and mail car to a point on the road three miles away, from which I could carry them down to the cottage on my back. But if the sea was rough or the road snowbound, no provisions arrived; and at low tide I would go and dig up cockles from the sand flats by some little islands at the edge of the bay, or tap limpets off the rocks. In prolonged wet weather, when Skye was blotted out from view and the waterfall ran in spate, it was impossible to dry out the driftwood, the only combustible fuel available, and the fire spat and hissed in the primitive range, filling the cottage with acrid blue smoke.

One day a boat came with a cargo of coal, but it drew too much water to come in close so the crew threw the coal—all 40 bags of it—into the sea, expecting I could gather it at low tide. The point where they dumped the coal was deep water, however, a sandy-bottomed region much favoured by scallops and starfish and only uncovered at the lowest of spring tides. It was several weeks before I could reach the spot. By then the bags had burst open and successive tides had washed most of the coal round the bay and the islands and into the mouth of the burn. Months later I was still picking up lumps that had been worn into porous black balls by the action of the sea—freaks of instant geology.

One definition of a wilderness is a place where a man might find it difficult to survive not only physically but also mentally. This was certainly true of Camusfearna in winter. The prolonged isolation, the short days and winter weather began to have an effect on me. I began to revert to an earlier, more atavistic way of life. I showed signs of going into a kind of human hibernation, retiring to bed earlier and earlier and getting up later and later. Above all I rediscovered my fear of the dark, a fear I thought had disappeared with my childhood. There was no piped water and no sanitation of any kind at Camusfearna. The burn, running swiftly over smooth boulders, made up for the lack of both facilities. But although it curved round the house barely a hundred yards away, after dark it filled me with dread.

On wild black nights I would take a hurricane lamp and an axe with me if I had to visit the stream. The axe was to defend myself against the nameless terrors of the dark; the lamp cast a protective circle of yellow light around me, lighting up the sodden ferns and the claw-like alders and turning them into an illusory zariba. There, in the most vulnerable of ordinary human situations, I experienced the same, naked animal fear our ancestors must have known when they strayed into the darkness from the security of the cave. Panic would rise in me like a fever. No effort of will, no appeal to reason could control this infantile dread. What did I fear? I could not say. It had no name, no face. It was the primeval snarl, the sudden leap, the fangs at my throat. It was wolf and werewolf, monster and beast. In the heart of such terror lies some clue to man's early relationship with the wilderness that surrounded him, and some explanation of contemporary man's attitude to the wild places he has not yet exorcized and tamed.

By contrast there were times when Camusfearna seemed the most beautiful place I had ever known. When a high-pressure ridge passed over, the skies often had a brilliant, crystalline translucency. At night every star glittered, Venus pulsed with white light, and Mars hung low over Loch Hourn and winked successively red, green and white. Sometimes shooting stars fizzed briefly through the night sky, and once—far away to the north-west in the direction of Greenland—I saw the cosmic, gossamer drapes of Aurora Borealis, the Northern Lights.

In such still, breathless weather, visibility seemed to be limited only by the curvature of the earth. I could see even the water-courses and the erosion scars on the high basalt cliffs of Eigg, whose eastern promontory, as a result of the mirage-like effects of refraction, seemed to have detached itself from the sea altogether and floated in a state of miraculous suspension. Sounds, too, carried over enormous distances. No traffic noise, no sounds of people en masse muddied the aural environment of Camusfearna. I could hear an otter scratch itself 200 yards away. From far out in the bay I could hear the splash of a dolphin leaping and the sport of a grey seal surfacing to breathe—sounds as hard as diamonds. On some evenings I could hear the stags roaring from far across the channel among the hills of Skye. The plop and rattle of every tired wave that slumped on the beach was clear to me, every heron kraak, every raven croak.

As winter deepened, snow began to fall at Camusfearna. One morning I found the burn frozen over, its rocky boulders sealed together with a patina of bluish ice that was cracked like the glaze of old porcelain. I spent most mornings accompanying the otters on their expeditions along the shore or to the deep pools below the waterfalls. There they could swim and dive, and often they would find something to eat, a shanny in the bladder-wrack and sea cabbage, or once a two-foot long conger eel, which disgorged an undigested, six-inch dab. At the seaward end of the burn there was a steep bank of compact sand where sand

In the bay of Camusfearna, on the West Highland coast of Scotland, the Atlantic surf provides a natural playground for Teko, one of the otters kept there by the late naturalist Gavin Maxwell and once looked after by the author. This deserted shoreline on the far north-west frontier of Europe is one of the few remaining wilderness areas that lie scattered across this most populated and man-dominated of continents.

martins nested in summer, and here the otters had built a slide. They had an infinite capacity for play, these otters, and for hours on end they would toboggan head-first down the slide into the water. Now that the water was frozen over, this game was doubly popular, for the ice extended the slide still further.

At the slide an incident occurred that taught me an important lesson about living in wild places. The male otter, the heftier of the two, had a habit—one among many—of standing on his hind legs and pushing with all his weight against the back of my knees. Usually the strength of my legs was a match for the weight of his body. But on this occasion I was caught off balance. As I struggled to keep a footing, the top of the bank crumbled away and I found myself hurtling down the slide towards the frozen burn. My gumbooted heels broke through the ice, followed by my legs and my torso up to my chest, and tumbling after me came a wildly excited otter.

No sound escaped my lips. Only the otter spoke. He squeaked and chirruped all around me. With his rubbery fingers he pulled on my left earlobe, stuck a grey luterine thumb up my nostril, gathered my lower lip in his fist and tugged on it, stood on my shoulder and pushed down on my head with all his strength—anything to complete my abrupt metamorphosis from terrestrial man to aquatic man, from bi-pedal master to four-limbed playmate. With stoic fortitude I stumbled to the far bank. Later, squatting in a Victorian hip bath in front of a fire of broken herring boxes, I reflected on the problems confronting civilized man in a primitive wilderness.

As a lonely representative of the species *Homo sapiens* at Camusfearna I lived a life as encapsulated as an astronaut on the moon. I wore a watch which told me when it was morning and when it was afternoon, when I should eat and when I should go to sleep. I carried about with me the thinking of a civilized background which sought to persuade me that man was the supreme species on earth and the only species in heaven. I turned for knowledge to written words, ignoring what was written in the rocks and what I could learn in the changing pattern of sea and sky and seasons, and in the lives of the living forms that shared this patch of the planet with me.

But if a man wanted to live in a wilderness, I realized, he should adapt to it, not fight it. This lesson sank home when the storm finally broke. The forecast had said the storm was imminent, but it did not arrive until the early hours. The wind did not work up strength gradually; it was at full strength when it came. It fell upon the house as decisively as an iron ball at a demolition site. Its percussive impact woke me. The door burst open and the sheets of my book manuscript were scattered derisively in the air. The fireplace belched soot like a steam train. The whole place juddered and boomed as the wind screamed in from the ocean and fell upon Camusfearna in fury. When dawn broke, a dull subterranean light filtered through the windows. The wind had whipped the spume off the sea in frothy bales and rolled them up the beach, collecting sand and dead seaweed as they went, until at the top of the beach it had hurled them like soiled snowballs at the house. Now the house was cocooned in a kind of sandy brown candy-floss.

For two days the storm raged. Some gusts must have reached almost hurricane strength. The corrugated roof of a ruined croft was torn away and hurled across the countryside like a scythe. Even the birds were grounded. I watched a heron trying to gain the shelter of a lee cliff, tacking this way and that against the wind until it grew tired and was borne backwards at breakneck speed in the direction from which it had come. To walk in such a wind was impossible. The otters were defeated by it, too, in spite of their streamlined shape. The wind would take hold of them and roll them slowly over on their sides. The only way they could proceed was to inch forward cautiously on their bellies with their legs splayed out, like newts.

On the third day, with the wind blowing fitfully under a steely sky,

I consciously gave up. I abandoned my book. I turned my back on my timetables and work programmes and put my watch in a drawer. I had joined the ecosystem. Such was my introduction to the wild places of Europe, to the first one I ever encountered in that continent—the few square miles of incomparable rock and water called Camusfearna.

After several months at Camusfearna, I made a rare foray and climbed to the top of Ben Sgreol at whose foot my cottage lay. It was a fine day, bright but cold, and I clambered up over scree and frozen snow, past tarns where great northern divers laboured into the air like flying-boats, and over tundra slopes where the stags in rut stared and roared, and ptarmigan in white winter plumage clattered from cover. I reached the summit in the early afternoon and peered about me in the clean dry air.

Now I was able to place my winter quarters in their geographical context. To the north-west were the snow-covered peaks of the Cuillins and the Red Hills of Skye, to the west the great whale-back hump of Rum, and beyond them the grey shapes of the Outer Hebrides. To the south and east lay mile after mile of eroded mountains and valleys devoid of human habitation. As for Camusfearna, 3,200 feet below, it had shrunk to the size of a table napkin, and I could hardly see the cottage, it was so diminished by the immensity of that lonely Highland landscape.

Living at Camusfearna my vision of the world had become blinkered, but this view from Ben Sgreol opened my mind to the extent of the land-mass on whose far north-western frontier I stood. Beyond the immediate peaks, beyond Druim Fada and Slat Bheinn and Gulvain, there lay a great hinterland that stretched across forests and plains and glaciers and marshes to the Volga and the very gates of Asia. As I stood on that modest, snow-capped summit, my legs braced against the fitful wind, my ears burning with cold, I tried to form a picture in my mind of that complex continent of Europe of which I and the stags and ptarmigans formed such a bewilderingly insignificant part. It was not an easy task. Like most Europeans, I found I had only the haziest idea of the layout of my own continent. Whole rivers and mountain ranges refused to fall into place, although their names were familiar. Where exactly did the Douro and the Vltava flow? Where precisely were the Cantabrian Mountains and the Tatras? I did not know for sure, and it took a lot of subsequent travelling and map-reading before the picture became clear.

I learned, for example, that Europe is not strictly a continent at all but a peninsula of Asia, jutting into the Atlantic Ocean and bounded to the north by the Arctic Ocean and to the south by the Mediterranean Sea.

Beyond shaded moors and sunlit foothills, Suilven Peak, 2,400 feet high, stands shrouded in low clouds typical of the Scottish Highlands. A relic of the ancient Caledonian mountain range, the peak's modest bulk of sandstone and quartzite is the end result of at least 600 million years of weathering.

Viewed as a peninsula, Europe is huge: four million square miles of land, enclosed on three sides by an exceptionally long (because exceptionally indented) coastline stretching for 50,000 miles. However, because Europe has had such a powerful and distinctive civilization, and is conveniently marked off on the fourth side by the line of the Ural Mountains, it has popularly been regarded as a continent in its own right—a geopolitical continent, rather than a geographical one. Viewed as a continent, Europe is small—less than half the size of the Soviet Union. Of the world's continents, only Australia is smaller.

I have now travelled over the boundaries of Europe from many different directions and in many different ways. My journeys have helped me to define Europe—that is to say, to examine with my own eyes the perimeter of this continent, to impress its outline on my mind. I have seen the black and mournful crags of North Cape, Europe's most northerly frontier, looming out of the fractured Arctic pack ice off the desolate Norwegian shore. In a steamer westward-bound from Suez I have voyaged under a roasting sky along Europe's southern borders and watched with sadness over my deck quoits and gin as migrating thrushes, low over the water, tried to cover the narrow gap that separates Europe from Africa at the Straits of Gibraltar, and one by one fell exhausted into the sea, where they fluttered and twitched among the waves and then lay still—sodden brown bundles that were sucked into the ship's propellors and mercifully extinguished from sight.

In a Soviet jet hurtling towards the Ural Mountains and Siberia I have peered down at Europe's eastern limits: the grey land ocean of the Russian steppes, darkening at last as the late midsummer sun sank towards the convex horizon. I was playing chess with a Red Army colonel and I could see camp fires of fur hunters and mineral prospectors burning in the woods far below.

"See, English!" the colonel said. "Now we say Europe bye-bye."

And I looked down and saw the dark stain of the Urals spreading away to the north, and later a myriad of tiny circular lakes winking the red sun back at me like a million distress signals.

"See, English!" the colonel said again, happily sliding his queen across the chess board. "Now we say Asia hello—and checkmate!"

To comprehend at a glance the physical layout of the interior of Europe, I would require a far higher vantage point than my perch on Ben Sgreol or my Ilyushin jet over the U.S.S.R. Only a spacecraft on an incredibly cloudless day would do. But if I imagined myself in such an exalted position, looking down among my weightless pellets of shrimp cocktail and banana pudding as I orbited over Europe, what would I see?

I would see in the north-west the worn-down remnants of the Caledonian range of mountains, stretching from Ireland to the Scottish Highlands and Scandinavia. South of these mountains I would see the great expanse of the European plains, beginning in the Low Countries, crossing northern Germany into Poland and reaching into the vastness of western Russia. Farther south I would see the eroded uplands of the so-called Hercynian ranges, extending in a great boomerang shape from the high mesetas of the Iberian peninsula up through the Massif Central and Vosges of France, round into the Black Forest and Harz Mountains of Germany and the Bohemian massif of Czechoslovakia, and east as far as the Lysa Gora plateau in Poland. Then, across the girdle of Europe, I would see an almost unbroken belt of high mountains running from the shores of the Atlantic eastwards to the Caucasus.

These are the Alpine or young fold mountains whose central and highest portion, the Alps, constitute the dominant physical feature of Europe. Offshoots of the Alps extend westwards, where the Pyrenees and the Cantabrians traverse the northern extremity of Spain; southwards, where they form the Apennine Mountains of Italy and Sierra Nevada of Spain; south-eastwards, where they form the rugged heights of Yugoslavia and the Balkans; and eastwards, where they form the half-moon of the Carpathians running through Czechoslovakia, Poland, the western Ukraine and Romania. Tucked within the protective area of the Carpathians lie the great grass plains of Hungary, called the *puszta*.

The Alpine mountains are the most recently formed in Europe and began to rise about 60 million years ago when, as part of the continuing changes in the earth's unstable crust, the continent of Africa started to drift northwards. As a result the Mediterranean basin was squeezed down to its present size and the southern edge of the primordial European landmass was buckled and folded, forming the Alps and their related ranges. This herculean upheaval was accompanied by earthquakes and salvoes of volcanic explosion; and because the process that formed the Alps has not ceased, those mountains are still rising, and volcanoes and earthquakes have continued to convulse the Mediterranean world in modern times. Eighty thousand people were killed when an earthquake flattened the Sicilian town of Messina in 1908, and there are still active volcanoes in Europe, notably Vesuvius near Naples, Etna in Sicily and, just to the north, Stromboli in the Lipari Islands.

I have never experienced an earthquake or a volcanic eruption in

Europe, but over the greater part of the continent the most striking formative agent in recent geological time has been ice rather than fire, and during my travels I have been able to observe and explore many ice-formed landscapes. Today the continent is like a battlefield littered with the debris of conflict after the armies have moved off—the aftermath of the last great Ice Age, which lasted more than two million years and drew to a close only 10,000 years ago. During that period the continental ice sheet advanced from Scandinavia to engulf most of northern Europe, and at its maximum extent buried one and a half million square miles as far south as a line between London and Berlin under a layer of ice up to a mile thick. The Alps were also heavily ice-bound, and sent out glaciers as far as the valley of the River Po.

Changes in the world's climate caused this ice cover to advance and retreat several times, so that in reality the Ice Age comprises several ice ages—at least five, perhaps more—alternating with long, warm interglacial periods in which plant and animal life slowly returned to the land that the ice had vacated. The ebb and flow of this colossal weight of ice was like the action of an immense carpenter's plane. It honed the rocks of Europe, grooved the plateaux, carved the peaks. And when 10,000 years ago it had withdrawn, it left behind a landscape characteristic of most of the continent today: huge moraines in the north, smaller ones in the Alps, drumlins of rocky detritus swept into neat heaps and dams, long chains of lakes trapped in the hollowed-out glacier beds, wide U-shaped valleys scoured by the glaciers, deep caves bored by the meltwaters, and a rich loess soil on the plains—the result of fine dust blown and washed down from the rugged regions of glacial debris.

Even now parts of northern Europe have a glacial climate that prevents the recovery of plant and animal life, and other parts are still in the grip of ice. In Norway a large proportion of the land surface is stark, bare rock, and the Jostedal ice sheet—60 miles long and 15 miles wide, the largest in Europe—still spawns glaciers and presents an all too vivid picture of how Europe once looked and how it may look again when the present interglacial period ends and a new ice age begins. In the Alps a quarter of the land surface lies under permanent snow and ice, a frozen reservoir more than half a mile thick in places that provides the source of Europe's major rivers: the Rhine, Rhône, Danube and Po.

Elsewhere in Europe the retreat of the ice allowed plant and animal life to take hold in the newly exposed areas of tundra, marshland and immensely fertile virgin soils. Pioneer trees such as birch and willow began the process of recolonization. As the weather warmed, whole

Amid clouds of gas and smoke, a flow of molten lava scorches its way down a slope of Sicily's Mount Etna, the largest active volcano in Europe.

belts of vegetation moved north until at the end of the Ice Age four main zones were broadly spread across the continent. In the far north was tundra; in the north (and on the mountains) there were dense coniferous forests; in the temperate latitudes encompassing the greatest part of Europe grew a vast deciduous forest of oak, elm and lime; and in the Mediterranean region, which had never been glaciated, there was a mixed deciduous and evergreen forest.

Compared with what it is now, Europe at the end of the Ice Age was a wilderness of astonishing luxuriance and diversity. From the River Shannon to the River Volga, from the Lofoten Islands to the Dodecanese, lay a haphazard pattern of swamps, forests, moors, mountains, caverns, islands, steppes, sea cliffs and meadows—habitats colonized by creatures from the south and east in an abundance that is unimaginable today. Among those creatures was one species of predator whose success was soon to eclipse the fortunes of all others—the primate known as *Homo sapiens*, or man.

If I pause for a moment and try to collect my thoughts about Europe, gather the bits and pieces of my personal experience gained travelling hither and thither across it over the years, I realize my dominant concept is one of enclosure. By comparison, if I think of Africa, my concept is one of space. I think of a day I got lost in the vast grass sea of the Serengeti Plains. Hour after hour I drove in new directions, but always I found myself circling back on my tracks, until I realized I was simply following the sun. There is nothing like that in Europe. In Europe there always seem to be signs of human presence when you round the bend in the track—a house, a fence, a noticeboard, an enclosure. Once, travelling alone in a remote part of the huge and desolate marshes of the Danube Delta, I found a Dutchman photographing *me* as I photographed a pelican. During a low-level flight over England, I crossed a singularly desolate and windswept stretch of northern coastline far from anywhere, and there among the dunes I saw a pair of lovers, frozen in the act by the aeroplane's clattering arrival overhead, their faces averted from the sky and clutching each other for cover as the little aircraft circled once, waggled its wings and retired discreetly out to sea. For Europe is not only a small continent; it is also the most densely populated in the world, with a population 70 times Australia's, ten times Africa's and seven times North America's.

It is impossible to talk about wild Europe without talking about man, for in no other continent in the world have his works produced such extensive changes in nature. The earliest Neanderthal hunter-gatherers

The edge of a snowfield beneath Norway's Jostedal ice cap has been undermined by summer meltwaters plunging down a rocky mountainside. Similar scenes were common all across northern Europe 10,000 years ago, as the Ice Age drew to its close and plants took hold in newly exposed landscapes.

in Europe a hundred thousand years ago made little impact on the natural world around them. They killed almost anything, from mammoths to toads, but lived in balance with their environment and could neither displace rival predators nor dominate other species. Partly this was due to their tiny numbers, estimated at between four and one hundred persons per thousand square miles, a density less than that of the Amerindian population of the Amazon rain forest today; partly it was also due to their puny technology. But 35,000 to 40,000 years ago a particularly refined version of the human animal arrived in Europe. Cro-Magnon man, as he is called, was *Homo sapiens* like us—a quick learner and a skilled hunter.

His impact on the animal world was catastrophic. Over the succeeding millennia a wave of extinctions swept across Europe. One by one individual species and whole genera vanished. In all, 50 per cent of Europe's larger animals became extinct following the advent of modern man, including the mammoth, the woolly rhino, Merck's rhino, the straight-tusked elephant, the great elk, the steppe bison, the cave bear, the cave lion, the scimitar cat, the spotted cave hyena, the Saiga antelope and the leopard.

It used to be thought simply that climatic changes killed off the big game in Europe. But similar waves of extinction followed the advent of modern man in other parts of the world as well, and it is now evident that man played a very significant part in these extinctions. Partly he had this effect by direct action, using his more advanced weapons and hunting skills; partly by indirect action, nudging the more vulnerable species towards oblivion by crowding them in their habitat or destroying their grazing grounds. At any rate, these little groups of hunter-gatherers to-ing and fro-ing all over Europe began to play an increasing role in the ecosystem and to exert an increasing dominance over the wilderness. As their numbers swelled they displayed a growing tendency to destroy the natural life of any region in which they dwelt, a tendency for which a new name has been invented: biocide.

One aspect of biocide is undoubtedly a pure killer instinct. I remember a particularly striking example of this instinct from my own experience and, although it did not take place in Europe, it was perpetrated by Europeans. At the time I was a young infantry subaltern in an African regiment in Uganda. Our unit was based near the strategically important source of the White Nile and one day two of my fellow officers took a Bren light machine-gun down to the banks of the river, where a large group of hippopotamuses lived. While one of the men crouched down,

A noctule bat, common in Europe's temperate woodlands, goes into a steep dive during a pre-dawn hunt. It navigates in the dark by sending out ultrasonic pulses and then monitoring the echoes. With this highly refined system it can detect flying insects, and catches them in the manner shown here.

the other rested the tripod legs of the gun on his back and began to empty magazine after magazine in rapid fire into the bodies of the help-less hippopotamuses until the water was blood-coloured. The men laughed; they ran about, firing as they went; their eyes blazed with al-most demonic excitement. Man the tiger, I thought then; man the slayer.

In Europe the large-scale killing of animals continues. For so long nature has been thought to be boundlessly abundant, its plants and animals the product of some divinely replenished cornucopia, that the old traditions of the rider to hounds, the stalker and falconer, tracker and trapper, poacher, beagler, courser and sporting scourge of flesh, fish and fowl have been slow to disappear. In Italy, two million licensed hunters—an army greater than the combined military forces of Britain, France and Germany, with an average fire-power of seven guns per square mile of hunting land—generally slaughter up to 200 million migrating birds every year, and when there are no more birds left they blaze away at butterflies and bats.

More revolutionary in its effects than modern man's undoubted killer instinct, however, was his skill in clearing and cultivating the soil. The techniques of agriculture were brought in from the east by Neolithic man between 6,000 and 7,000 B.C. and by the time of Homer they were established through a great part of the continent. Vast stretches of the forests of southern and middle Europe were felled and burned by the new farmers, who sowed their crops of grain and pulses in the fertile ashes. In the clearings around their forest settlements these little peasant communities grazed the domesticated progeny of the animals they had once hunted, and declared war on the carnivores—the wolves, bears and lynx—that preyed on their stock. Then, as the soil gave out, they moved on to clear and burn more of the forest.

For the first time man was no longer dependent on the vagaries of a wild environment for his food. The result was population growth on an astonishing scale. From as little as four people per hundred square miles the population density of Europe went up to a thousand in the early stages of the agricultural revolution and now, after the industrial revolution, with all its unprecedented wealth and security, it is over 25,000 per hundred square miles.

There were few natural checks to the changes that such large numbers of people with increasingly sophisticated technology at their command could bring about over the face of Europe, and the wilderness fell back. Many species of the plant and animal world, their habitat modified or their breeding grounds disturbed, managed to find refuge in the few remaining wild places; many others were decimated or exterminated.

Europe is now in large measure what man has made it; and yet, considering what the landscape has endured at the hands of man, it is surprising not how few wild places are left, but how many. In part this is due to a change of heart in the last decade or so, to the recognition that man is an animal, that he survives biologically or not at all, that his biological survival requires the survival of other species and those species require a stable environment to support them, a wild place they can call their own. There are now hundreds of protected areas scattered throughout Europe, from huge national parks like the one at Stora Sjofallet in northern Sweden covering nearly 600 square miles, to conservation areas, nature reserves and bird sanctuaries as tiny as Bass Rock in the North Sea.

But not all national parks are wild places and not all wild places are national parks. So what, in the context of Europe, is a wild place? In my opinion it should be as near as possible a primordial piece of our planet, neither permanently inhabited nor modified by man—a place you enter in a spirit of wonder and humility, a place where the living forms grow free and unfettered according to their own natural laws, where the balance of nature is undisturbed. Second, it should be a place where, without support from outside, a man would seriously doubt his own survival, but where at the same time he might find the freedom of space and silence and solitude, and discover a new relationship with the earth and all living things, a relationship which some Amazon Indians still have and which our forest ancestors once knew.

For a place to fulfil such criteria, it must be sufficiently large or (if it is small, like an island) sufficiently remote for signs of the intensively developed human civilization encircling it not to be evident. Where are such regions to be found in Europe? The answer almost invariably is in two sorts of places: in country that is too unproductive or inaccessible for developers or farmers to bother with, or country that has been out of bounds to most people for a long time, usually because it was the private hunting ground of kings or noblemen.

Such wilderness areas lie scattered across Europe like oases in the desert of human development. They vary greatly in kind: from the snowfields of the high mountains, where no life exists, to the marshlands of the great river estuaries, where birds congregate in their tens of thousands; from the vegetable gloom of primeval forest to the scorching plains and eroded wastelands of the Mediterranean.

Excluding Russia and Scandinavia, which are covered elsewhere in this series, I approached the wilderness areas in radial fashion, starting roughly in the centre of Europe with the Alps, the fiercest and grandest wild place of all, and moving outwards and downwards until I came to the frontiers of the continent: the coasts and offshore islands. Because the wild places of Europe are so localized and so far-flung, I made no attempt to describe them all but instead set out at various times of year to visit areas each representative of a type—highland, woodland, dryland, wetland, island—and in all these places I found the hallmark of a true wilderness: they were all in varying degrees hostile to man.

Within its protective ring of water the tiny wilderness at Camusfearna tolerated man only on sufferance. Beneath the tangled thickets of gorse and bramble it was still possible to detect the foundations of stone huts where a small fishing and crofting community had tried to eke out a subsistence a hundred or more years before. They had retired defeated and no one had ventured to take their place. Until recently an old fisherman had survived alone in a croft on the far side of a sea loch only a few miles away. But when I went there in the dinghy one calm day I found the old man had gone, too, and there were deer in his overgrown garden and two hinds in his tumbledown parlour.

Now it was my turn to leave. The spring had come, the sun had reappeared over the hills, the geese were flying back from the south. Soon the elvers from the Sargasso Sea would swarm up the burn, and the sand martins from Africa would nest again in their holes in the bank. If my ears had been more sensitive, I would have heard, above the ceaseless murmur of the falls, the agitated bustle of spring, the uncoiling of fern and circulation of sap, the chrysalids stirring and the earth alive.

I left Camusfearna with mixed feelings, for I was substituting this wilderness for another in a different continent. When eventually I returned again to the wild places of Europe, it was to a region very different from the windswept West Highlands, and in an antiquated form of transport highly appropriate to the exploration of a primeval wilderness.

The Hidden Survivors

Of all Europe's wild creatures, it is the small and seemingly defenceless insects that have proved to be unrivalled masters in the art of survival. Where other and much bigger creatures died out long ago or hang on in pathetically reduced numbers, the insects flourish. The reason for their success is their adaptability in the face of disaster. Under constant threat in Europe from predators and man, many make use of camouflage to avoid detection and attack. And so neatly do some of them blend with their natural surroundings, disguised as leaves, sticks and tree bark, that they can go unnoticed by even the most keen-eyed observers. Their larvae also rely on camouflage, and although the disguise may bear no resemblance to that of the adult, it is usually equally effective.

How did such insects acquire their disguises? Probably the process was started by the appearance within a species of some mutants bearing a random resemblance to an aspect of their environment. The more these escaped the notice of predators, the more opportunity they had to breed and pass on their life-saving traits to their descendants. In time, such traits came to characterize the species as a whole.

This process goes on in Europe today. Colour-adaptation by the peppered moth, a common woodland insect, has provided what one eminent geneticist has called "the most striking example of evolution which has ever been witnessed in any living organism, plant or animal". The normal variety of this moth has white wings peppered with black specks, which enable it to blend with tree bark and lichen. But during the 19th Century a blackish peppered moth became predominant in and around the grimy industrial areas. Made conspicuous by the soot-blackened background, the lighter variety was easier prey, and as its numbers thinned the darker kind came to the fore. But now, with cleaner air, the lighter variety of moth is making a comeback.

Deceptive shapes and colours, however, will be useless to an insect unless it remains completely still. Camouflaged surfaces therefore tend to be those that are displayed in a resting position. Since most butterflies settle with their wings pressed vertically together, the undersides of the wings are disguised. But most moths rest with their wings folded downwards like a tent and so the upper surfaces are camouflaged.

Rendered almost invisible by its colour and immobility, an immature grasshopper suns itself on a Hungarian gentian. The widely varying colour patterns of grasshoppers are well developed only in adulthood, but the nymphs in their more uniform, pale shades merge nicely with the flowers and grasses of summer backgrounds.

In its imitation of a twig, the larva of a large thorn moth (left) creates a baffling camouflage, even appearing to bear the scars of old foliage. It stretches from the real twig at the bottom of the picture to the leaf at the top left, and with its two pairs of hind legs and three pairs of forelegs, it can hold on like this for many hours.

The larva of a lappet moth (right) moulds itself into the shape of its resting place, using minute hairs and tissue on its flanks to fill in the join and smooth out any shadow that might betray the presence of a rounded body. Its rough, rusty back matches the colour of hedgerow twigs on which it feeds and later hibernates.

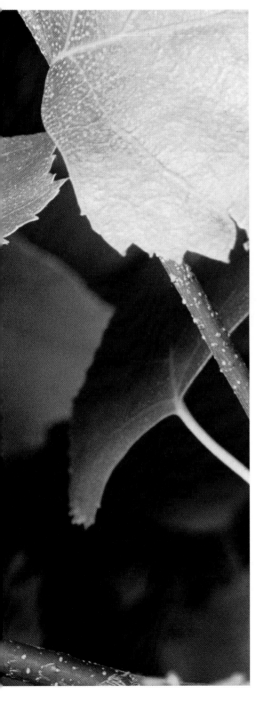

Whether it is seen from the side (left) or head-on (above), the buff tip moth is almost indistinguishable from a snapped-off fragment of dead stick. Its lichen-patterned wings merge readily with tree-trunks, and the pale patches on its wing-tips confuse its real contours and give the impression of a broken end by suggesting three dimensions on a two-dimensional surface.

The adult lappet moth (above) can hardly be distinguished from the bunch of dead leaves it is resting on. So expert is its disguise that it even simulates a stalk with the long sense-organ protruding beyond its head. But the deception can work only while the moth remains in its resting position, with the forewings folded over the hind pair to compose a suitable pattern, and the edge of one forewing simulating the midrib of the leaf.

A brimstone butterfly (right) shows the underside of its wings, coloured, shaped and veined to look like the green leaves of its woodland environment. The upper surfaces of its wings, a bright, conspicuous yellow, are completely hidden when it is at rest. It feeds and breeds only on buckthorn, where its early hatching larvae are perfectly camouflaged by displaying the paler shade of young buckthorn foliage.

The night-flying yellow underwing moth finds almost perfect concealment against the mottled bark of a tree, its habitual daytime resting place. If it is disturbed, its yellow underwings flash as it zigzags away, startling and confusing predators, until it settles on some other natural resting place. It then refolds its patterned forewings and merges once again into its surroundings.

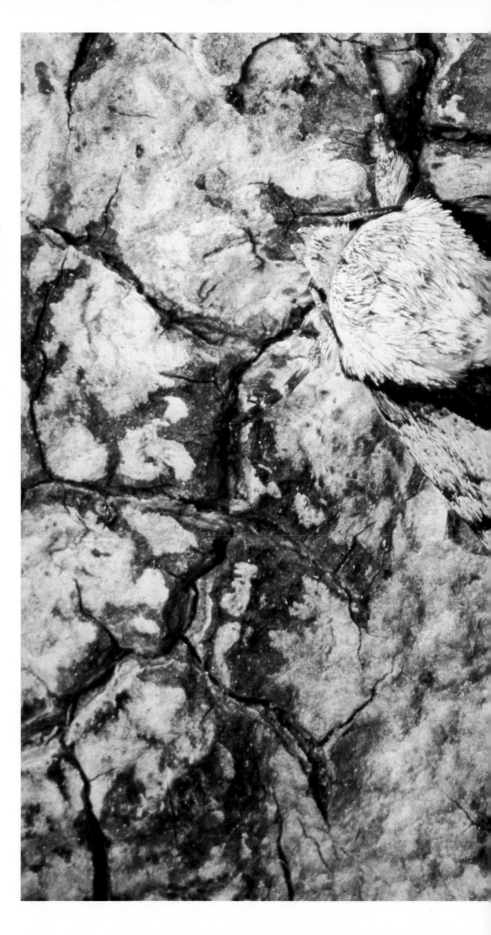

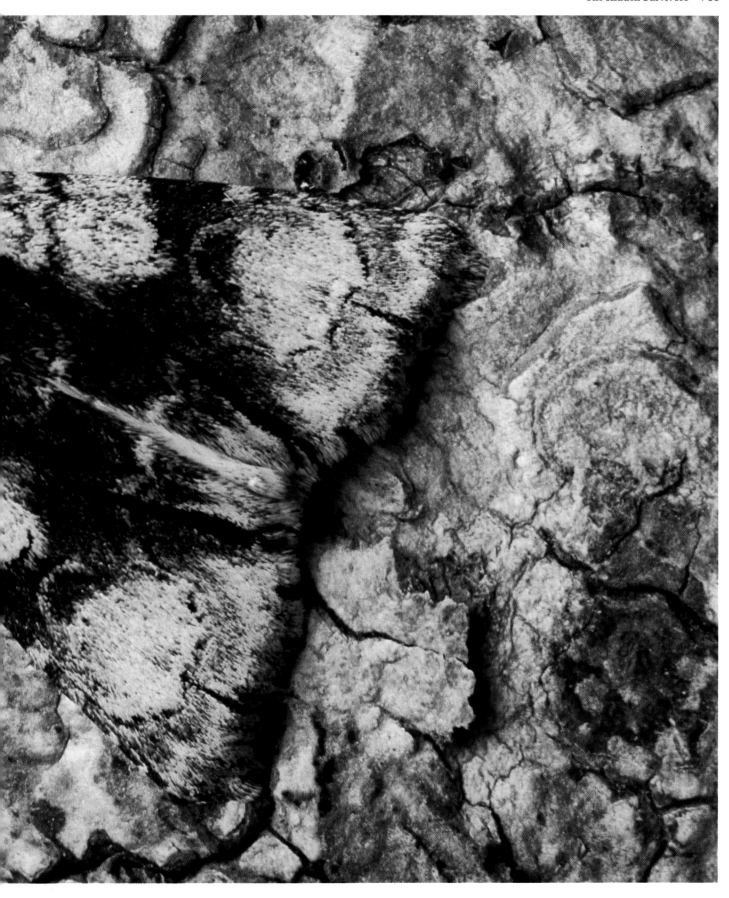

2/ Over the High Alps

The soul is uplifted, the powers of intelligence seem to widen, and in the midst of this majestic silence one seems to hear the voice of Nature and to become the confidant of its most secret workings.   HORACE BÉNÉDICT DE SAUSSURE/VOYAGES DANS LES ALPES

I was awakened at half-past four in the morning by a banging on my door and a voice in the darkness calling, "Get up, Doug. The weather's good and we're going to go." It was an unholy time, an hour or two before dawn; the world beyond my bedroom window was black and silent and no wind soughed in the fir trees. I had slept intermittently, waking every hour and lying in the darkness contemplating the day that lay ahead of me. It was not so much fear that disturbed me, as curiosity, for there was nothing I could do to change the course of events now. When the knuckles of my friend's fist beat reveille on my door, I knew that in a couple of hours I would be entrusting myself to the upper airstreams in a contraption of wicker, manilla rope and rubberized cotton full of inflammable hydrogen, and that by mid-morning I would be dangling nearly 20,000 feet above the central Alpine ranges of Switzerland.

My impending balloon flight over the Alps was an indirect result of my winter at Camusfearna. One of the few people to visit me there was the traveller and science writer, Anthony Smith. Together we had worked out plans for a balloon safari across East Africa, with the object of observing the annual game migrations from the air, and a little more than a year later we made our aerial crossing of the plains and forests of Tanzania. Our orange and silver balloon was called *Jambo* (which is Swahili for "Hello"), and it was *Jambo*, a little patched and darned after her African experience, that Anthony and I eventually brought to the

Swiss Alpine village of Mürren, 5,500 feet up in the Bernese Oberland, beneath the snow-capped peaks of the Mönch, Eiger and Jungfrau.

For several years an annual trans-Alpine ballooning week had been held at Mürren. Situated in the middle of the wildest and most extensive ranges of the Alps, the village was an ideal point for us to start from; for whichever way the wind blew it would blow our balloon over a primordial wilderness where the Ice Age still lingers, a territory beyond the reach of human activity and hostile to life of any kind. Our aim was to fly as far as we could, making a film record of what we saw and savouring something of the spirit of the high Alps.

There is no better way of comprehending the great mass of the Alps than from the air, and no better vehicle than a slow, silent balloon with its 360° field of vision. A balloon is part of the Alpine environment in a way an aeroplane or a helicopter is not. The mountains subject it to the vagaries of their airstreams—and they mete out their own rough justice, as I was soon to discover, when the hubristic balloon pilot resumes his mortal status at the moment of touch-down. The hazards are obvious enough: the glaciers, ridges, snowfields and scree slopes of the highest mountain range in western Europe are not an ideal landing ground for any airborne craft; and a balloon, which can go only where the wind blows, is liable to land anywhere. I knew that balloonists from Mürren had floated off in every direction—to Germany, to France, to Italy, to Liechtenstein and to Austria—and although no one had yet been hurt ballooning over the Alps, the possibility was always present.

Anthony was the pilot and it was therefore upon his shoulders that the responsibility of the flight fell. A balloon pilot has a limited number of ways he can control his balloon. He can throw out sand ballast to go up, he can release gas to come down. Because at different altitudes the winds often blow in different directions, he can exert some control over his direction by ascending or descending to a new airstream. Beyond that he must rely on quick reactions and a knowledge of local conditions.

Every day Anthony attended pilots' briefings conducted by Fred Dolder, the doyen of Alpine balloonists and organizer of the annual ballooning week. Never take off with fewer than six 30-pound sacks of sand ballast on board, Fred explained, or you may run out too soon (we took off with five, since *Jambo* proved too small to lift more). Never try to land in a valley, or the convection currents will blow you out again (but we did try, and the currents did blow us out, just as he had said). Don't fly above 20,000 feet, or you will suffer from lack of oxygen. Don't fly below 14,000 feet or you may bump into an Alp. Make sure you land in time to climb down a mountain before nightfall. And don't forget your walking sticks: you will need them on the mountainside.

Anthony and I punctiliously remembered our walking sticks. At 7.30 a.m., with the light from the still-hidden sun gleaming on the white ridges of the Breithorn to the south-west, we hooked the sticks on the edge of our wicker basket and clambered on board. It was a perfect morning—the sky cloudless, the air stable, the wind moderate. *Jambo's* hydrogen-filled envelope swayed gently above our heads. Near by, the two balloons that would accompany us were given final checks before they, too, were ready for take-off.

"Have you got your walking sticks?" Fred Dolder shouted. "Have you got your sticking plasters, cold chicken, compass, passport, hunting horn? Are you sure you have no matches or cigarette lighters?"

"Yes," we replied.

"Then will you go now, please."

Anthony removed some of the sandbags that weighted down the balloon but *Jambo* failed to rise. Another bag was taken out, leaving only five.

"Hands off!" said Anthony in English.

The ground crew took their hands off the basket. In a second or two their upturned faces diminished appreciably in size.

"*Gute Reise!*" bawled the rapidly receding Fred. "Good trip!"

"Rule Britannia," sang a group of bystanders, presumably British.

We were off. The question was, where to? The winds at ground level indicated an easterly course. But where would the upper airstreams carry us? The possibilities were considerable. The Alps reach 750 miles from east to west, a long white semi-circle of mountains stretching from Nice to Vienna and cutting off Italy from the rest of Europe; they also stretch as much as 155 miles from north to south. In all, the Alps cover nearly 80,000 square miles, an area equal to two-thirds of Italy.

As we rose from Mürren, the panorama of the Bernese Oberland began to spread out around us. Our silent, effortless levitation above the expanding snowscape was exhilarating, but for a moment it seemed the flight might not go on at all. We were drifting east-north-east towards the most forbidding of the peaks that glowered over Mürren—heading, in fact, directly towards the gaunt peak of the Eiger.

In order not to collide with the mountain, which rises to just over 13,000 feet, we had to climb at an extremely rapid rate. Anthony threw out more handfuls of grey, gritty sand ballast and the balloon rose faster. The black circle of the balloon's shadow on the ground

Seen from the summit of the Aiguille de Triolet in the French Alps, ice-chiselled peaks rise like islands above a mile-high sea of strato-cumulus clouds. In the distance, some 35 miles to the south-east, are the heights of Italy's Gran Paradiso mountains, beyond which the Alps begin their descent towards the River Po.

diminished to a dot, then vanished altogether as we began to cross the
great gash of the Lauterbrunnen Valley. Our two companion balloons,
flown by German pilots, floated silently up beneath us like bubbles
through the thin air. The chalets of Mürren dwindled to starboard.
(Or was it larboard?) The balloon was turning slowly, like a top, so that
first we were facing one way, then another. Neither of us spoke as we
corkscrewed towards the Eiger.

The Eiger is one of the most notorious peaks in Europe. Its most
villainous part is the North Face, a 5,000-foot triangular wall of cold
black rock, frequently ice-covered, constantly bombarded by falling
stones. The North Face had long been considered unclimbable, and it
was not scaled until 1936, after a series of spectacular disasters. By
1970 more than 250 people had climbed it and 40 had died there.

The wind bore us not over the top of the Eiger but just to the north of
it. We drifted past the North Face, still ascending rapidly, and peered
down at the sunless wall of rock and ice with morbid curiosity. As our
eyes grew accustomed to the scale of the mountain, we were able to pick
out small details, and our gaze fastened upon two orange-coloured
shapes, equipped with legs and arms, about half way up the summit
triangle and quite close together—mountaineers in orange anoraks.
The climbers made no movement of foot or hand or head, and we
realized that they were not climbing on the rock face at all but hanging
from it by their ropes—they were motionless not because they were
resting but because they were dead. We learned later they were
Spanish climbers who had died there a few days previously. As we
looked at them, there was a loud explosion above our heads and for an
instant our hearts stopped beating.

Tethered just above our heads in the rigging of *Jambo's* basket were
half a dozen toy balloons which we intended to release during the flight
to find out the direction of the winds above us. During our rapid climb
from Mürren we had forgotten about them, but as the altitude increased
and the atmospheric pressure dropped, the gas inside them had
expanded, so that when we reached the dead Spanish climbers the
balloons were huge and bloated and could stretch no more. When the
first exploded, we assumed *Jambo* itself had torn open—and we carried
no parachutes. We cut loose all the toy balloons, but they floated
upwards and were caught in the netting overhead where they continued
to blow up one by one, most disconcertingly, for the next half hour.

By the time we left the Eiger behind us we had reached 14,500 feet
and were still climbing. We were now higher than any of the neigh-

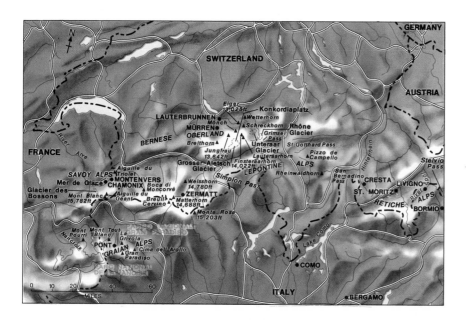

Within the great curve of the Alps straddling France, Switzerland and Italy lie the highest points of Europe outside the Caucasus. The region of eternal snow (areas in white on the map) lies above 9,000 feet; the treeless tundra or Alpine zone (grey) occurs above about 6,500 feet; numerous fertile valleys are found above 1,500 feet (brown); below that are found river meadows and lowland plains (green).

bouring peaks. Indeed, within a few minutes we were higher than any part of the European continent outside the U.S.S.R. and for the first time we had an unrestricted view of the Alps from our balloon basket. It was a sight without parallel in my experience. There was not a single cloud, not a drop of moisture in that dry, royal-blue Alpine sky. At 8 a.m. the rays of the sun were still low enough to model every peak and even the most distant ranges stood out sharply. Anthony and I had a radius of vision that included the great mass of the western and central Alps and stretched as far as the great peaks of the Matterhorn and Monte Rosa to the south and the Mont Blanc Massif to the west.

Immediately to the west were the great ramparts of the Jungfrau. Its plunging, semi-circular eastern wall falls sheer towards the 2,300-foot-deep ice reservoir of the Konkordiaplatz, which feeds the principal glaciers of this part of the Alps—among them the 14-mile-long Grosser Aletsch glacier, one of the longest in the Alps. Ahead of us lay a formidable line of peaks, the central battlements of the Oberland—the Wetterhorn, Schreckhorn, Lauteraarhorn, and Finsteraarhorn; and against these giants lapped a whole ocean of lesser peaks and ridges and glaciers and icefields—a vast sea whose waves seemed to have petrified into rock and ice.

Twelve miles north-east of the Eiger, near the snowfields surrounding the Schreckhorn, the wind veered a few points southward. It was now blowing to the east-south-east at some 20 miles an hour. Finally our flight path began to level off at about 18,000 feet. In getting to this altitude we had already expended two of our five precious sacks of sand and we were well into the third, but, assuming the sand ballast lasted and the wind continued to blow as it did, we could reckon to reach Italy in the region of Bormio in about four to five hours.

We settled down to enjoy the ride. Strung out a mile or two behind us —sometimes higher than ourselves, sometimes lower, but borne along on the same steady airstream—came our two companion balloons. Big bubbles of gas in pretty red-and-yellow striped bags, they seemed to float perilously near the most formidable razor-back crags or sink horrendously into the sunless chasms that yawned between the peaks; but always they floated upwards out of trouble. We felt grateful for their company, for now we were flying over a wilderness as empty and seemingly as limitless as the Antarctic plateau. It was a fantasy world of dazzling white snow and deep blue sky, made all the more fantastic by our own unreal passage across it.

Man has been settled in the Alpine valleys since the Stone Age, and as much as 50 per cent of Switzerland's rugged terrain is forested or under cultivation. But wherever we looked we saw no sign of human habitation—no roads, no resorts, no ski-lifts or cable-cars. This region of the Bernese Oberland lies, in the main, above 9,000 feet, the average limit of permanent snow in the Swiss Alps. We looked down on a pristine, untouched and utterly silent world. In most places, because sounds travelling upwards meet no obstruction, it is possible for balloonists to hear the faintest terrestrial noise with a clarity far greater than that experienced at ground level—every chicken squawk or dog bark or child shout reaches the balloon basket as clear as a bell. But from these frozen wilds no sound of any sort reached up to us; for there was no form of life to utter any. This absolute silence—a very rare experience in ordinary life—reduced Anthony and me to relative speechlessness; when we did speak it was *sotto voce*, as if we were in a cathedral and did not wish to be overheard. Otherwise there was nothing but the creaking of wicker, the tap of the pilot's knuckles on the altimeter glass, the whirr of a movie camera.

We continued to fly at 18,000 feet most of the time, but occasionally we exceeded that height. Since we were not acclimatized to the thin air we began to suffer from lack of oxygen, although we did not fully realize it at the time. Ordinary tasks became more difficult and took a lot of time—the result of oxygen deficiency in the brain. I spent a full

Not far below the snowline—at a height of perhaps 6,000 feet—a carline thistle hugs the rocky earth of an Alpine slope. The plant grows well in the conditions of drought, cold and strong wind found at such altitudes. Its hundreds of tiny flowers, packed tightly together in a thistle-like head, are protected by the spiny leaves and the rosette of slender, silvery bracts.

30 minutes sitting in the bottom of the basket with my hands in a film-changing bag trying to reload the magazine of the outboard movie camera, a task of a few minutes in normal circumstances. My sense of time deserted me, so that when we sat down to breakfast I believed it was lunch time, and indeed continued to believe so until I checked the pilot's map a few days before writing this chapter, and found the real times entered at various checkpoints.

Breakfast, I see from that map, was served at 9.20 a.m., after we had crossed the foot of the four and a half-mile long Rhône glacier, the source of the Rhône River near the Grimsel Pass, and after we had flown over St. Gotthard Pass and drifted over the Pizzo de Campello in the Leventine Alps. Perhaps I could be excused for confusing it with lunch, for when we finally extricated our food from the tangle of sandbags and equipment in the bottom of the basket, it proved to be a baronial spread. We raised a little folding table, laid a cloth over it and set down a whole cold capon, a string of frankfurters, a long French loaf, a round of Camembert cheese, one bunch of bananas and one of grapes, a bottle of champagne, two glasses and a little vase of Alpine flowers.

The champagne was like ice, for the temperature of the air around us was 10° F at this altitude—22° below freezing. However, because a balloon travels with the wind—is part of that wind—there was no passage of air to chill us, and in the strong ultraviolet sunlight we felt warm.

We finished our meal half an hour later as we passed over the ice-fields and glaciers of the Rheinwaldhorn where the eastern tributary of the Rhine has its source. We flew over this stream, the Hinterrhein, at the point where the precipitate road from the San Bernadino Pass zigzags down to meet it, and floated eastwards for two more utterly dreamlike hours. At last signs of man were becoming more frequent: more roads in the valleys; the white concrete arc of a dam like a drawn bow; the blinding flash of a green hydro-electric lake as it winked back the sun to us. In place of our precious sand ballast, we threw out the remains of our meal—manna from heaven for some marmot or chough below—and watched as they sank through space and vanished from sight. The mountains were no longer quite so high or so white. Many of the peaks had no snow on their summits; the dark greens of the fir forests and the light greens of the meadows became more frequent.

Our thoughts began to turn from the infinite to the finite. We began to think about our landing. We had now been airborne in our basket for five hours. Our sand had lasted well, after all, and we still had two sacks left. But the full breadth of northern Italy now lay ahead of us only a quarter of an hour away; and although the central Alps were beginning to peter out, we could see new high ranges in our path some way off—the peaks of the Dolomites rising blue on the horizon. We no longer had sufficient ballast to surmount these obstacles. We drank the remains of our champagne and, because of the shortage of ballast, tossed the bottle overboard to lighten the balloon. The tinkle of glass on rock came back to us long afterwards. Then we made ready to land.

A mile or two beyond the Italian border lies the village of Livigno, the highest village in Europe, strung out along the steep, narrow valley of the Spöl. We decided to come down there. Anthony pulled long and hard on the valve line to release gas, and we began to descend. We began to spin. Gusts of air hit us in the face. There was the sound of flapping fabric above our heads and the basket creaked loudly. More hissing of gas from the valve at the top of the balloon, more cold wind blustering around us, the feeling that things were not quite right, a twinge of concern. The mountains revolved slowly around us. The valley floor drew nearer—a road, houses, terra firma, help. The raw, hard, all too real surface of the Alps, over which we had floated so arrogantly, was now only a few hundred feet below us; the balloonist's moment of nemesis was drawing near.

We failed to descend far into that valley: the convection currents threw us out. Then, when the updraught stopped, we plummeted at nearly ten feet a second towards a precipice at the edge of the snowline on the mountainside overlooking the village. The balloon's shadow, which I had last seen receding from us near Mürren, now reappeared advancing towards us near Livigno. Foolhardily, I filmed it as it grew larger and larger. It grew larger very rapidly and I was still filming it when it hit me in the eye. My movie camera was driven against my forehead, my forehead in turn drove it lens-first through the stout wickerwork of the basket. There was a flash inside my head and a moment of oblivion. Then nothing but an immense sound of grasshoppers, chirruping in the sun and confirming the fact of my continued existence.

So ended our five-hour aerial voyage across a hundred miles of the Alps between Switzerland and Italy—and the longest-seeming and most extraordinary morning I have ever spent in my life.

3/ At the Edge of the Snowline

Nowhere is this beauty more strikingly revealed than in the mountains. For there flowers bloom among dead wastes of rock, close to regions of eternal ice. . . . They grow in a world of frost and heat, cold and drought, avalanche and hurricane.

VOLKMAR VARESCHI AND ERNST KRAUSE/ *MOUNTAINS IN FLOWER*

My balloon flight over the Alps had provided me with an unparalleled view of one of Europe's largest wild places. From my wicker gondola I had been able to turn my gaze through 360° and look out over nearly 50,000 square miles of high mountains. The flight had served to show that many regions of the Alps are still *désert* and *sauvage*—as pristine and austere as on the day of their creation. But the only physical contact I had had with those wild regions was my collision with the mountain-side above the Italian village of Livigno.

So hard and headlong was this contact that it gained me the unwelcome distinction of becoming the first and only person to have been hurt in a trans-Alpine balloon flight. My forehead was deeply gashed, my knee twisted, my brain mildly concussed. When eventually I was carried down the mountain on the back of a diminutive member of the Alpine rescue service—my legs flopping about, as Anthony described it later, like those of some nursery giraffe—I could not tell what time of day it was, nor what day of the week, let alone take in my surroundings.

To get to know the Alps at all intimately, to feel their pulse and smell their breath, so to speak, I needed to stand on the flanks of a few of them at my leisure, to get down on my hands and knees and peer at them more closely. I needed above all to see what I could not see from a balloon —the characteristics of the Alps' living forms and the action of the Alps' physical forces, their glaciers, meltwaters, avalanches, streams. The best place to conduct such an exploration, I considered, was the rough and uninhabited zone between about 5,000 and 9,000 feet, where the forests of spruces, firs, larches and pines give way to the Alpine meadows and stretches of open tundra that reach up to the line of eternal snow. For much of the year these rugged uplands are covered in snow and ice, but it is here in spring and early summer that the characteristic flora of the Alps achieves its greatest beauty and variety.

Travel in the Alpine zone can never be taken lightly. Although the flora and fauna are well adapted to the environment, man can survive only artificially in the shelter of widely scattered climbers' huts or ski centres. At night or in bad weather, the vicinity of even these high-altitude oases can be hostile, and a man can die of a fall or perish in sub-zero temperatures within a few hundred yards of a warm bunk and a roaring stove. There is a danger, too, of falling into a crevasse in a glacier. At least 1,200 glaciers still grind their way down Alpine valleys, and although they are small compared with their Ice Age predecessors, 300 are more than four miles long, and in Switzerland they account for 5 per cent—or 800 square miles—of the land surface.

My return to the Alps, therefore, involved a series of forays, a collection of core samples from a few specially selected areas. Some of the least spoiled regions of the Alps are national parks, and I decided to aim for two of the finest: the Gran Paradiso in Italy and the Vanoise in France, which are adjacent to each other and noted for their rich Alpine flora and fauna, especially their herds of rare mountain goats, the chamois and ibex. On the way I planned to visit two of the highest and most famous peaks in Europe: Mont Blanc and the Matterhorn.

So, one day in May, in the company of an old friend of mine, Brian Featherstone, an Englishman who works as a shepherd in the Provençal Alps and knows the mountains, I set off. Normally May is springtime in the high Alps, but we encountered the most wintry spring weather in living memory. The unseasonal snow, with its avalanches and blocked passes, served to make the Alpine wilderness wilder still, so that our travels were at times difficult and on occasion even dangerous.

One of my reasons for visiting Mont Blanc was to explore the 8-mile-long Mer de Glace and its tributaries, the longest glacier system on the mountain and the fourth biggest in the Alps. But when Brian and I arrived at Chamonix at the foot of the mountain, the clouds were so low they almost touched the valley floor. Of Mont Blanc, or the Aiguille du Midi or the other towering peaks, there was no sign. Nor was there any sign of the Mer de Glace. As we ascended towards the mistbound glacier, we passed from drizzle to blizzard. The climb towards the edge of the glacier was hazardous in the extreme. We had to cross a slippery snow slope that plunged downwards into the mist. Out of that mist came terrible noises—the grinding and crunching of the invisible glacier as it moved its immense burden of ice down into the valley. I stared into the cold grey mist, but I could see nothing. I could only listen as crevasses opened and closed with a noise like falling coal.

I had better luck the next day, when the cloud lifted a little and I was able to have a look at one of Mont Blanc's shorter and steeper glaciers, the Glacier des Bossons. It was a frightening sight. On the skyline huge blocks of ice the size of houses and double-decker buses were poised to tumble down from the ice-field above. Below me, where the glacier ground slowly over rock-steps into a steep, tree-lined valley, there was a wild jumble of formidable *séracs* or ice-towers. Farther down, the surface of the glacier was deeply scarred with blue-green crevasses.

The Glacier des Bossons has a certain distinction in the history of glaciology, having provided some important clues to one of the main questions concerning glaciers—that is, their rate of flow. Normally ice is too brittle to flow, but under sufficient pressure it will behave like a plastic material and flow in much the same way that tar does. In a glacier the lower levels are under enormous pressure from the weight above, and that pressure is continually increased as snow falls on the upper slopes and the snowflakes gradually coalesce to form new ice. As a result the glacier moves downhill, its surface torn apart by crevasses as it flows unevenly over the valley floor. On steeper slopes the rate of flow naturally tends to be faster, but even the fastest-flowing glaciers normally move too slowly for the human eye to see. Consequently it is necessary to have markers of some sort for observation; and it was in this respect that the Glacier des Bossons proved helpful, thanks largely to various unfortunate human beings who perished within its crevasses.

In 1820 members of a mountaineering expedition were swept away by an avalanche when they were within a thousand feet of the summit of Mont Blanc. In 1861 their bodies emerged from the snout of the Glacier des Bossons, having descended 10,384 feet during the intervening 41 years—a rate of $8\frac{1}{2}$ inches a day. Five years later an English climber fell to his death on the same mountain. In 1897 his body, too, appeared at the snout of the glacier, and calculations of his rate of descent confirmed the rate of the glacier's movement.

An even odder case occurred more recently on the Weisshorn in Switzerland. In the summer of 1955 the perfectly preserved body of a young man was ejected from a glacier at the foot of the mountain. At first he was thought to be a Swiss who had fallen to his death ten years previously. But his clothes were rather oddly cut, and later he was identified as a 19-year-old German climber who had been caught in an avalanche on the Weisshorn in 1888. It had taken him 67 years to travel one mile down the glacier—exceptionally slow progress, since the average rate for Alpine glaciers is one mile every $11\frac{1}{2}$ years.

There is no figure for the number of people killed in the Alps—not only those who were swallowed up in crevasses, but also those who were swept away by avalanches, overtaken by darkness or blizzards, or who simply got lost and died of hypothermia on the snowfields. But no other area of Europe except the sea can have cost so many lives. It is hardly surprising that for many centuries Europeans regarded high mountains as horrible, ugly and dangerous places. Only in the late 18th Century did opinions change. The French writer Jean-Jacques Rousseau idealized the mountains as symbols of the savage nobility of nature, so eroding the view that they were horrible and ugly; and the Swiss physicist Horace Bénédict de Saussure demonstrated that they were not necessarily dangerous either.

Saussure was the first patron of the modern art of mountaineering. He combined a romantic passion for the Alps with a restless desire to discover the scientific secrets they might hold. "It is above all by studying the mountains that we can speed up the progress towards a theory of the earth," he asserted. In particular, he was anxious to conduct a series of tests at high altitude on the electrical charge of the atmosphere, and its humidity and temperature. In 1760 he took the first step towards the realization of this objective, and offered a prize to anyone willing to risk his life by climbing to the summit of Mont Blanc. Given the 18th-Century lack of mountaineering know-how, an attempt to climb Mont Blanc then appeared as daunting as a space shot today. Twenty-six years passed before anyone set out to claim the reward. In 1786 a crystal hunter, Jacques Balmat, and a doctor, Michel Paccard, both of Chamonix, successfully made the ascent with few safety precautions—they did not even link themselves together with ropes. Saussure was overjoyed at their success and a year later, accompanied by Balmat, he himself made the climb and successfully conducted his pioneering experiments.

Other scientists followed Saussure's lead and the early part of the 19th Century saw many hardy academics pursuing their researches among the glaciers and peaks of the high Alps. These men were the true

TOURISTS AND GUIDES POSING ON AN ICE PINNACLE

Victorians in the Alps

Mountaineering emerged as a phenomenon of 19th-Century Europe. Originally the eccentric pursuit of a handful of enthusiasts, it later became a fashionable activity for privileged travellers. By the 1870s and 1880s, when these photographs were taken, short, guided tours into the snow were a commonplace of Alpine tourism, even for timid visitors.

Mont Blanc, the highest peak of the Alps, and the first to attract keen climbers, had been ascended as early as 1786. Serious mountaineers soon turned their attention to other Alpine summits that offered greater challenge, but even in the late 19th Century the unsophisticated public was still responding to the lure of the famous peak.

For the fit and hardy tourist there was a guided ascent to the summit—more a demanding walk than a real climb. But most parties (like the groups striking their attitudes in the pictures to right and left) contented themselves with a day on one of the spectacular glaciers that descend the mountain some 10,000 feet below the summit, within easy reach of the comforts and pleasures of Chamonix.

LADY MOUNTAINEER AND COMPANIONS ON THE GLACIER DES BOSSONS

explorers of an unknown European interior. The new world they opened up was so extraordinary and so exhilarating that they began to climb for fun as well as science. In part the attraction was sport and adventure, in part it was an affair of the human spirit: no man loves life more than when he is in danger of losing it, and in few other places is a man more intensely aware of spiritual values than among the lonely peaks of the high mountains. And so mountaineering became a craze in Europe, and the conquest of the Alps gathered pace. In the mid-19th Century—the so-called golden age of Alpine mountaineering—European climbers, predominantly British, conquered every single major peak in the Alps. One of the significant events in this period was Edward Whymper's ill-fated ascent of the Matterhorn in 1865 during which four members of his team were killed. The mountain has been invested with an aura of notoriety ever since.

I went to see the Matterhorn as people go to see the Mona Lisa or the Pyramids or the Changing of the Guard. It was one of the great mountain legends of the world, like Everest, or Cotopaxi, or the Mountains of the Moon. When Brian Featherstone and I left Mont Blanc the weather was still bad, but soon after we arrived near the base of the Matterhorn on the Italian side, the clouds dispersed briefly. There ahead of us stood the peak, this great tilted slab of snow-covered gneiss, one of the most dramatic mountain profiles in the world. The Matterhorn is a unique obelisk of a mountain with four steep faces, and until Whymper's ascent, it was believed to be unclimbable.

Whymper had tried eight times to climb the Matterhorn from the Italian side and failed on each occasion. On his ninth attempt, when he was 26 years of age, he approached it from the Swiss side. Viewed from ground level at Zermatt the peak looks almost vertical, but close at hand the angle of slope is seen to be only 40°. Whymper and his six companions reached the summit easily. But during the descent one of the climbers slipped, dislodging three others. Whymper and the remaining climbers felt a violent tug and then nothing. The rope linking them all had snapped. "For a few seconds," wrote Whymper afterwards, "we saw our unfortunate companions sliding downwards on their backs, spreading out their hands, endeavouring to save themselves. They passed from our sight uninjured, disappeared one by one, and fell from precipice to precipice on to the Matterhorn glacier below, a distance of nearly 4,000 feet. So perished our comrades!"

It was rumoured in Alpine circles that Whymper had cut the rope to save himself from being pulled after the four doomed men. But later it

Protected against the harsh Alpine winter by its chestnut-brown coat, a sure-footed chamois stands poised among the snow and ice of its mountain habitat. Its only concession to the heavy seasonal snow is to move down from its high eyries to meadows where it can feed on shrubs and lichens.

was discovered that the rope had been their third best, meant for emergencies only. Somehow it had been muddled up with their best one. Since that historic accident more than 100,000 people have climbed the Matterhorn, including a 76-year-old man and a seven-year-old girl; and in 1950 a four-month-old kitten made a solo climb to the summit and was brought down by a guide who found it there next day. But more than a hundred people have lost their lives on the mountain.

I did no mountaineering in the Alps, but on the first day I ventured into the Gran Paradiso range, 30 miles to the south-east of Mont Blanc, I came near to grief. It was 6 in the evening when Brian and I arrived at Pont—an inn and a few houses at the head of a splendid, U-shaped valley below the Gran Paradiso, the 13,320-foot peak after which the national park is named. For the first time the sky was clear. But there was a huge accumulation of snow, and the snowline reached down to the valley floor. It should have been obvious to us that a climb up the Gran Paradiso without skis was going to be arduous, not to say dangerous in view of the lateness of the hour. But we were full of euphoria that evening; and the invigorating air of the hills, the sense of space and freedom this landscape gave us, caused us to overlook two cardinal rules of the mountains: we failed to tell anyone where we were going and we failed to ask anyone about local conditions.

Our aim was to spend the night at a refuge high on the mountain, and explore outwards from there the next day. We loaded our rucksacks with what we called essentials, including weighty tomes on ornithology and Alpine flora, and a bottle of scotch—articles I was bitterly to regret within half an hour—and set off in a spirit of cheerful endeavour. It was a fine evening, still and clear. The great peaks loomed silent and virginal all around us and I had the illusion of entering the limitless interior of some uninhabited continent.

At first all augured well. Our route took us along the side of a rushing little stream called the Savara. On top of a vast round boulder by the bank, I spotted a chamois. It stood in profile, clearly outlined against a patch of snow on the slope behind. It was so motionless, so symbolically posed, that for a moment I thought it was stuffed—a heraldic effigy to mark the portals of the park whose boundary we were approaching. As we came closer the creature turned its head and gave us a fixed, un-embarrassed stare. I had not seen a chamois before and through my binoculars I carefully studied its goat-like, gazelle form, its distinctive little hook-tipped horns, its cream and chocolate coat, its alert and delicate mien. Then I stumbled and sank up to my knees in a drift of snow and when I recovered and looked back the boulder was empty. Apart from a sparrow hawk quartering down the valley, the chamois was the last wild creature I saw that day, the last thing I had any energy to look at.

The refuge we were climbing towards was at a height of nearly 9,000 feet between two glaciers, the Gran Paradiso and the Moncorvé. It was 2,500 feet above our starting point; the first 1,500 feet had to be climbed in a horizontal distance of just over half a mile—a gradient of one in two. This would have been exhausting enough under normal weather conditions; but the track was covered in fresh snow up to two or three feet deep, so that each step up required double the effort. My pack weighed about 40 pounds and soon felt insupportably heavy. Before long the completion of each step, the lifting of the lower foot to join its mate higher up, became a triumph of the will.

Three days ago I had been living a sedentary existence in London and for weeks I had been laid low by a succession of virus infections. I told myself all this, excused myself to myself when I found all the strength gone from my legs, when I stood bent double fighting for breath, staring blankly into the landscape that had become, for the moment, hateful to me. Brian, who lived in a hill village with streets so steep that even to go to the baker for bread was like a commando exercise, regarded my Alpine prowess with some concern. Unacclimatized, convalescent, overweight, underpowered, I pressed on behind him, step by painful step. The snow grew deeper, the track steeper, my need to rest more frequent.

And so we reached the point of no return, 1,300 feet above the valley, half way in distance and time. It was here that a party of three Germans overtook us. They looked efficient. They had grey glacier cream round their mouths and red skis on their feet. They passed us without a nod or a word. We stumbled behind, plunging one foot into the deep snow, taking a breath, then extricating the other foot. There did not seem to be much future in this. It was already 8 o'clock, the temperature was dropping fast and the sweat on my shirt felt as chill as ice.

We were saved from our predicament by a twinge of conscience on the part of the youngest of the Germans. He stopped above us and hailed the leading member of his party. They conversed briefly while the man in front remained facing forward, ski sticks held ready, impatient to go on. Then the younger man turned to address us.

"You must be careful!" he shouted.

We nodded weakly. Yes, we must.

"This is fresh deep snow," the German continued. "It is easy for us on skis, but it will be very hard for you. It will be dark at 9 and I think you will not arrive until 10 maybe. You will have to follow our tracks in the dark and you may lose your way. Then you will be in a very dangerous situation. You will come to some harm. But if you turn back now you will be down by dark."

Brian and I conferred. The German was right. If we were caught out on the bare mountain at night, we would probably be dead by morning.

"It is up to you," shouted the German. "I tell you what I think."

Too tired to speak, I pointed my thumb downwards. We thanked the German and turned round. Relieved of the agonizing burden of gravity, we descended swiftly. We stumbled through snowdrifts, over slippery rocks, through muddy streams and across the soft brown needle floor of a pine wood. The western sky beyond the white-browed summit ridge of Mont Tout Blanc turned from flamingo pink to egg-shell blue.

"Look!" said my shepherd friend. "L'étoile des bergers—the shepherds' star."

Low down between two peaks, Venus shone with a brilliant incandescent light, a celestial oxy-acetylene glow in a pastel-coloured sky of cut-glass clarity. I looked at the glittering planet once, noted that it was beautiful, then returned my concentrated attention to our own planet at my feet. An exhausted man is an introverted man, his vision of the world is a most circumscribed one; the most I saw of this transection of the Gran Paradiso was a pair of brown boots crossing a moving background of snow, meltwater, Alpine rock, Alpine bog, mud and gravel. By 9 the valley was already dark and it was difficult to see our way over the last few hundred yards. We reached the inn. Six wooden steps led to a wooden verandah and the door to my room. On the fourth step I paused, fighting for breath. Then I slogged on up.

The next morning I awoke to find the sun in my eyes and the sound of bird-calls filling the air. The freak cold weather that had dogged my wanderings in the Alps so far had suddenly changed. I emerged blinking into a world miraculously transformed. The sky was deep blue and cloudless, the sun was hot, there was a bustle and scurry all around as the plants and animals of the Alps awoke to the first warm day of the year after eight months of winter. Instead of attempting to climb up the flanks of the Gran Paradiso again, a penance for which I no longer had the strength or inclination, we decided to climb up the mountainside on the other side of the Pont valley. By midday we had climbed to more than

7,000 feet and on a large, flat-topped boulder before a triangular peak called Cima dell'Arollo we stopped to eat lunch.

From where we sat on the rock we could see the refuge we had tried to reach the night before, a round-roofed structure like a polar cairn, and the snowfield we would have had to cross and on which we might have perished had we not turned back. There was a great deal of snow on that side of the valley; the slope there received little sunshine and was plunged in shade at an early hour in the afternoon. On this side of the valley, however, the sun beat down and the air was full of the sound of running water as the snowline receded and the meltwaters poured over every rock face and gurgled down every channel and seasonal stream-bed. The world sounded of cataracts, and each cataract had a different voice—piano or forte, bass or alto—according to the volume of water and the height of its fall.

I looked at a meltwater stream through a magnifying glass, peering into it with my nose barely an inch from the surface of the water. The tiny stream, one of a million such temporary water courses in the Gran Paradiso range, was full of minute grains of rock whirling down towards the valley below. These tiny fragments—the detritus of erosion from higher up the mountain, chipped and torn by frost and wind and rain from the great, solid-seeming peaks all around me—were of many different colours: pink, grey, green, rust and black. They represented parings from different kinds of metamorphosed Alpine rocks: schists, quartz and gneiss, with fragments of chlorite, talc and garnet.

The particles streamed endlessly past my narrow field of view on the first stage of their journey to their final destination: the silt flats and sediment-laden lagoons of the Po Delta on the Adriatic coast of Italy. The world in my glass was a tiny part of that grand metamorphosis whereby the sharp peaks of the Alps were being smoothed down and removed via the great drainage system of the Rhône, the Rhine, the Po and the Danube to the edge of Europe, to the flood plains and the sea.

Not only water was on the move. Yesterday I had seen nothing but a few closed and huddled gentians; otherwise the ground had seemed as lifeless as a slagheap. But today new flowers, single or in clumps, appeared at every turn. They covered the brown, tundra-like clearings in the snow with a patchwork of yellow and purple blossoms; they sprang out of the clefts in rocks, and peeped from the detritus of the winter ice. This was the beginning of the Alps' great seasonal miracle, when the plants make the most of the short growing season and the ground is covered with a brilliant carpet of flowers—yellow snow

Among the melting snows of the high Alps, a spiny pasque flower unfurls its petals in the April sunshine. It is one of the earliest plants to blossom in the mountains and is highly sensitive to changes in temperature and humidity—even half an hour of cloudy weather will prompt the protective outer petals to close.

buttercups, violet Alpine asters, dark blue gentians, light blue delphiniums, black yarrow, mountain flax, Alpine columbine, glacier crowfoot, primulas, campanulas, rhododendrons with masses of red and pink flowers and—in remote and secret ledges—the most famous Alpine flower of all, the silvery edelweiss.

The giant boulder on which I sat once more was both microcosm and macrocosm, both a tiny part of a whole and itself a whole made up of many other tiny parts. A passenger jet flew overhead at 30,000 feet, leaving a straight white vapour trail that drifted slowly south-west over the Boca de Montadeyne. If a passenger had looked away from his airline lunch and peered down to where I sat, a line projected from his eyeball would have bisected the boulder and passed right through me. But he would have seen neither the boulder nor me. Reduced by distance to infinitesimal proportions, we would have been absorbed into the whole complex pattern of white peaks and dark valleys.

And yet this big boulder was a world of its own. It was smooth and rounded, with a single deep groove worn in it and a number of parallel scratches running from the back to the front—the result of glacial erosion during the Ice Age. The rock was grey, with traces of cream coloured quartz in it, and patches of lichen covered parts of it like a scab. The predominant lichen was a pale green, which under my magnifying glass resembled inlaid enamelling : a compact scab of little green nodules with here and there a patch of grey and black ones (dead and dying parts, perhaps). There were other kinds of lichen on the rock: one was lead-coloured and shaped like the whorls of a human brain, another was rust-coloured and glowed fiercely. These primitive lichens were the first stage in the pastoralization of primeval rock, and helped to form a rudimentary soil in which more advanced plants would be able to grow.

Ants strode across the boulder, insect dromedaries in long caravans bearing foraged goods from the edge of the world, from the melting tundra of snow and ice where Brian and I dropped crumbs of bread and bits of sausage skin. One of the ants had carried a large crumb a distance of 30 feet, and it was now lodged fast in a jungle of short prickly grass that grew in a cleft in the rock. These clefts were the fertile valleys of the boulder desert. Soil of a kind had gathered in them, and various mosses had gained a footing, as well as some very small flowers. One of them—with broad, thick leaves like an artichoke—was already putting out mauve blossoms; but most of its flowers were still tightly furled like flags. Here and there the meagre soil of the cleft was fertilized by the droppings of herbivorous animals—ibex or chamois, or perhaps both.

The ibex and the chamois were the great set piece of the Alpine tableau around that boulder in the Gran Paradiso. I had hardly hoped to see so many of them and probably would not have done so if the lowness of the snowline had not forced them farther down the mountainside than was normal for that season. We had seen a few scattered individuals on our way up but now we were surrounded by 50 or more ibex in several groups—massively built mountain goats with hefty haunches and notched, scimitar-shaped horns up to three feet long. In spite of their bulk, ibex are astonishingly agile and can jump across a crevasse 20 feet wide and land on a ledge the size of a soup plate. The members of the herd were grazing quietly on slopes where the snow had partly melted, or basking in the sun beside a stream that tumbled over a cliff. Several were asleep, their heads turned round to rest on their rib cages. One had made himself comfortable on a fractured boulder, lying on a soft bed of moss with his back against the raised part of the fracture; the creature peered down the slope with a fixed stare so typical of ruminant animals and short-sighted humans. Three hundred feet above the ibex grazed a small herd of chamois—friskier and more graceful animals altogether.

Warm-blooded animals can combat the cold in three ways: by migration, by hibernation, or by seeking shelter. Chamois are migrators, moving down to the conifer forests when winter comes. Ibex, on the other hand, prefer to shelter in the lee of rocks or under snow ledges, and

A marmot emerges from its communal burrow high in the Swiss Alps to set about the business of the day: eating. During the brief summer, this two-foot-long rodent spends as many as five hours every day nibbling plants—storing up enough fat to last through its hibernation during the six to eight months of extreme cold.

only in exceptionally bad weather seek the haven of the woods lower down. Today there are about 5,000 ibex in the Gran Paradiso—a tribute to the protection given them over the last century and a half by the Italian crown and state. Sadly, other large Alpine animals, notably the predators, have had no such luck. The lynx has been exterminated from the Alps (although it may be reintroduced in the Vanoise). The wolf, too, is extinct in the Alps, although a few packs still exist in the Abruzzo National Park in the Apennines, where 80 to 100 bears, the largest European carnivores, also cling on, together with a few in the Dolomites and the Pyrenees.

My favourite Alpine creature is one of the smallest. The marmot is a furry, amiable, harmless, cuddly-looking rodent related to the wood-chuck of North America and the bobak marmot of the Siberian steppes. With its cream coloured tummy, its rich chocolate-brown coat, wispy beard, little articulated fingers, snub-nose, child-like face and piping danger call, the marmot is an endearing animal; in character a bit of a clown, a bit of a baby. Below the stream where the ibex whiled away their first warm afternoon of the year, a waterfall fell to a patch of grass riddled with burrows. Here a solitary marmot scuffled and sniffed, diving down one hole and emerging from another. In all probability it had only been awake for a day or two after an unusually prolonged winter sleep, for marmots escape cold by hibernation. As many as 15 share communal burrows ten feet deep and for six to eight months they remain comatose, with lowered temperature and metabolism, digesting their own fat. In summer they spend their day eating grass and wild flowers in the Alpine meadows.

Through my binoculars I watched the marmot's tail disappear down one hole, its snout appear from another, and then suddenly I saw the animal stiffen, raise itself on its hind legs and pause rigid with fear. A second later an immense cracking sound split the air, like a roll of thunder. I looked up towards the summit of Mont Tout Blanc, from which the explosion seemed to have come. But I saw nothing. An avalanche must have given way somewhere above us, but its descent had been out of our view. The conditions were ideal for avalanches—hot sun on a winter's thickness of snow—and not long afterwards a similar explosive sound came from the white slopes of the Gran Paradiso. An echo of almost cosmic proportions rumbled among the high peaks and then the mountain world was at peace again, silent but for the sound of falling water and the piping of marmots.

Avalanches, big or small, are an annual feature of the Alpine scene. They are an important factor in shaping the landscape of the Alps: when they fall, they smash everything in their path, so that tongues of bare land stretch deep into the woods. On this land the vegetation must pass through various stages of succession before it regains its lost territory.

There are many different kinds of avalanche: dry-snow and wet-snow avalanches, loose-snow avalanches falling from a single starting point, slab avalanches falling from a large front. The most spectacular type is the airborne powder avalanche, which may attain speeds of up to 225 m.p.h. and an impact pressure of 2,100 pounds per square foot. Such an avalanche can lift an iron-girder bridge or topple a 120-ton locomotive, and is accompanied by a hurricane-force wind which can pick up a man and throw him half a mile through the air. By contrast a wet-snow avalanche may move so slowly that a man can get out of its way; but it can be up to 100 feet thick and contain as much as two and a half million tons of snow, which solidifies like concrete when it has come to rest.

The day was passing. A wisp of cloud, like steam from a volcano, grew from the summit of the Boca di Moncorvé. The shadows on the western side of the valley grew darker. We packed our rucksacks, left our boulder—that world within a world—and began our descent. My face and arms were deeply burned by the sun and the rocks were warm to the touch. Two whistling marmots stood on their hind legs to watch us pass. I answered their whistles with a wolf-howl and they fell silent. I felt remarkably well.

I passed my last night in the Alps in a wooden refuge on the slopes of Mont Pourri, a 12,395-foot peak in the Vanoise National Park of the French Savoy Alps. It had been another day of bitter weather. Climbing up from the Nancroix valley, full of the sweet, homely aroma of cattle barns and woodsmoke, we passed through woods of dripping larches and thickets of stunted willows, and came to a crabbed and inhibiting world above the snowline, where signs of life were fleeting and elusive. A thick, cold mist swirled around us. Choughs on ragged wings soared and circled in and out of our vision. Wheatears and rock thrushes fluttered from nowhere to nowhere like phantoms, and the marmots piped in the mountain fog, warning each other of our approach.

The mountain hut was high up beneath a rock wall of tortured granite, beside a fast-running stream of icy water. There was no one else there, and we chopped wood, fetched water, lit the stove and poured ourselves a dram of whisky each. The weather was closing in fast and we felt as marooned as polar explorers. For the moment, we no longer had any connection with the world of men. The world around us was primeval, entirely governed by the forces of nature and inhabited by creatures who had no involvement with man.

The weather changed in the night. The mist had been dispersed by a cold air stream and when I awoke at half past four in the morning a clear moon was shining on the crags of the mountains. An Alpine accentor, sounding like a skylark, sang bravely somewhere below. The frost was deep, the snow as hard and brittle as glass. The peace in the mountains was absolute, the sense of space infinite. In a world of such primordial, almost ferocious purity, I had a feeling of staring down the throat of eternity, of the imminence of some revelation about man and the universe. At dawn the sky was as clear as crystal; the peaks and valleys of Mont Pourri as sharp in that transparent light as pebbles in a rock pool. I looked out at an immense view of the Plan de la Plagne, a glacial valley with a frozen lake at one end and an arch of cloud crossing it like a bridge at the other, and I began to comprehend those matter-of-fact and down-to-earth men who clambered among the wild Alps in days gone by and were moved by what they saw and felt to utterances of mystical and even prophetic portent.

Before we left Mont Pourri we recorded the date in the visitors' book of the refuge and wrote: "Douglas Botting, photo-reportage, Time-Life Books, London, and Brian Featherstone, shepherd, of Simiane La Rotonde, Alpes de Haute Provence, arrived from Gran Paradiso, departed by the normal route. Fog, snow, hail and rain. We salute the guardians of the Vanoise National Park."

It was only when I returned to civilization that I discovered that my trousers had no seat to them. Some perilous scrabble, some sudden slip of mine on ice or scree—and the Alps had taken their revenge once more.

Beasts at Bay

From the moment man appeared on the continent of Europe, he relentlessly fought and hunted its wild animals. Few people apart from the ancient Greeks made any serious or methodical attempt to study them until, in 1551, the Swiss naturalist Konrad Gesner published the first volume of his monumental four-volume work, *Historia Animalium.*

Challenging the fanciful and often superstitious notions of earlier writers, Gesner attempted a scientific classification of all animals then believed to exist. He illustrated his perceptive commentary with careful and detailed drawings, some of which are shown on these pages, accompanying photographs of the animals that still roam Europe's remaining wildernesses.

In Europe today many of the species so painstakingly enumerated by Gesner have been wiped out, or they exist only in sparse numbers. The Alpine ibex, for example, is now indigenous only to the Gran Paradiso National Park in Italy (although it has been reintroduced to other areas where it once used to range).

The fast-dwindling European lynx is confined to isolated areas mainly in northern and eastern Europe, and its last important southern stronghold, the Guadalquivir River delta in Spain, contains no more than 15 pairs of the Spanish sub-species.

Italian and French mountains shelter about 100 brown bears, and the whole continent may retain no more than 10,000 of these massive predators. Wolves were still common in parts of Europe until the beginning of the 19th Century, and the annual kill in France exceeded 10,000 as late as 1883. But the wolf is now reduced to small and isolated groups, scattered from Portugal to the Soviet Union.

Such other European animals as the boar, the red deer and the fox have fared better: paradoxically, the popularity of pursuing them for sport led long ago to their partial protection. (Gesner described various methods of hunting them.) As a result, the long-tusked, short-tempered boar still grubs for roots in varied habitats from Poland to Spain, while the fox has proliferated to become Europe's most common carnivore. Penalties for poaching red deer have worked so effectively that, in a further paradox, the creatures are now having to be intensively hunted to prevent them from destroying their forest habitats through sheer weight of numbers.

Like the creature drawn by the naturalist Konrad Gesner four centuries ago (above), today's European wild boar likes a muddy wallow. This one (right) is up to its snout in a pool in Germany's Odenwald forest. Gesner fancifully believed that the predilection for muddy areas shown by boars was not only to escape from their enemies, but also to lower their blood temperature, which, he wrote, is normally very high as befits their "ardent and fiery nature".

A lynx stalks through the snow of
southern Sweden (right), insulated
from the cold by its winter coat.
When Gesner did his drawing of the
lynx, he was unsure of the animal's
classification, but he did recognize
that it was "of the kind of cats",
since it was carnivorous, had good
eyesight and climbed well.

A herd of Alpine ibex streams across the Gran Paradiso mountains in Italy. Gesner was much impressed by the ibex's "admirable celerity".

Hunting at over 7,000 feet in the Swiss
Alps, a red fox (left) demonstrates its
ability to exist in habitats other than
its original woodland range. Gesner's
fox was longer and leaner—and the
naturalist noted that although basically
a carnivore, a hungry fox would devour
practically anything. This, together
with its "strength, courage and
policy", he wrote, helped to ensure its
abundant survival.

Defying all other males in the area, a majestic red stag (right) roars its autumn mating call through a Danish woodland. It is still not known whether the antlers are designed primarily for combat, for attracting hinds or for showing rank within a herd. But Gesner made them a dramatic feature of his drawing and indicated that each might bear as many as seven branches.

4/ Primeval Woods

One can go into the woods, not for brushwood and not for mushrooms, but just to go, for no reason, and hug two tree trunks: dear ones, you're all I need.

ALEXANDER SOLZHENITSYN/ *THE GULAG ARCHIPELAGO*

To see the deciduous woods of Europe, or what is left of them, one must descend from the coniferous zone of the mountains and enter the lowland plains that stretch from the Atlantic to the Urals. Deciduous forest was once the characteristic landscape of much of lowland Europe, and in its hey-day this forest of oak and other broad-leafed trees was almost as vast as the Amazon rain forest today. By 2000 B.C. it had achieved its greatest extent and glory, covering the British Isles, the southern parts of Scandinavia, France and northern Spain in the west, and reaching in a wedge shape into Russia in the east.

It was a self-regenerating, high-canopy forest in which the dominant trees formed a continuous upper layer above a lower layer of herbs, shrubs and young trees. Within the area of this prodigious tree cover, there were extensive bogs and marshes. Great rivers flowed down from the highlands through thick woods of willows and sallows, and meandered across flood meadows of magnificent luxuriance. In the tall, dark forest itself there were game trails and clearings made by the larger animals: the aurochs (half as big again as a Hereford bull), the bison, the elk, the wild horse, brown bear and red deer. It would have been a quiet, lonely and dangerous place, that primeval forest.

Today all but one or two small enclaves of the forest have been destroyed, but the minds of many millions of Europeans are still filled with the aura of those woods: with their annual rhythm of bud-burst and leaf-fall, and with their smaller creatures—fox, wolf, badger, owl—and their legends and demons. The ancestors of the present-day inhabitants of England, France, Belgium, Germany, Poland and Russia wove fairy tales from their forest experiences and their superstitions—tales like *Goldilocks, Hansel and Gretel, Little Red Riding Hood,* and sagas like the *Nibelungenlied,* which still survive as a living part of many Europeans' cultural heritage.

In retrospect my own childhood seems like the childhood of the European race. I have always imagined that I was brought up in the middle of a wood and gleaned a knowledge and an instinct for woodland life from years of intimate contact. In reality this was not so; at my most formative age I lived in the middle of a small town in the Yorkshire dales, to which I had been belatedly evacuated after the blitz on London during the Second World War. But for a year or two, a large part of my free time was spent in a fragment of the ancient Forest of Knaresborough—a wood of beech and fir, oak, holly and tangled rhododendron thickets bordering the open rolling dales. In that vestigial wood I learned the ways of the forest, learned to stalk, to freeze, to climb trees, make dens in the branches, forage for mushrooms, berries, crab apples, hips and haws, beechmast and hazelnuts, wild horseradish and the young fresh leaves of the hawthorn (which we called bread and cheese, and ate). Here I first set eyes on badgers, weasels and shrews, learned to tell the different birds apart, cut my hand on razor grass, fell out of a tree, and became aware, with the close proximity that only a child can know, of all the smells and feels and shapes and colours and movements and sounds of all the different wild things of the forest. For me that wood was a natural sanctuary from the adult world outside, its host of living forms an extension of the fantasy world of my inner self.

So long as the war went on, the wood was safe, for people had other things to do than chop it down and build it over. Sometimes, concealed at the edge of the wood, I would watch the bombers return from their night raids over Berlin and the Ruhr. Long after the main body of aeroplanes had passed by, damaged stragglers with oily smoke streaming from their wings came droning slowly over the fields of the dales, where the lapwings cried and the dippers bobbed in the beds of the streams and the bluebottles huzzahed in the cowpats.

One morning in early June I made a special journey to the wood to hear the dawn chorus, that remarkable early summer oratorio when every waking adult bird simultaneously stakes its verbal claim to its nesting territory. The last note of nightingale, blackcap and wood warbler had hardly died away before it was replaced by a distant and increasingly urgent growling roar. I ran through the wood, ducking and dodging in the growth of brambles and young ferns, while the roar in the sky grew louder. In time I came to an area of sandhills and rabbit warrens beside a deep blue pond we called (and believed to be) "the bottomless lake". Here the cover of the tree canopy was broken and I could look up into an unobscured sky, watching the great armada of aircraft flying over. They were American aeroplanes, with three white stripes round their fuselages, and many of them were towing big brown gliders that swayed lazily in the air behind them. It was the beginning of the Second Front, the invasion of fortress Europe.

When the aeroplanes had gone, it was very quiet. The rabbits stayed in their holes and no birds called. I never went back there much after that. A year later the war came to an end and eventually I left the district. Long afterwards I learned that the wood, with all its oaks and pines and beeches, had been chopped down, the ground bulldozed and an estate of little houses had been built on the site. I do not know what happened to the badgers and the shrews and the nightingales that had lived there. But, although the delicately balanced ecosystem had been utterly destroyed, no doubt some creatures had learned to adapt to their new environment of hedgerows and gardens, as individuals of so many species have had to do since the coming of agricultural man to the forests of Europe more than 8,000 years ago.

Anyone who took a train from the Hook of Holland to Moscow, as I once did, would find it difficult to believe that the land he was crossing had supported one of the greatest forests in the world. Everywhere there are plains, meadows, heaths, arable farmland; of trees there is hardly a sign —only scattered copses, occasional softwood plantations of fir and pine, a few groves of broad-leafed trees on steep slopes where no plough can reach them. But a little to the north of that east-bound track, out of sight of the Soviet railway carriage with its samovar and heroic music, lies an exception. One hundred and fifty-five miles east of Warsaw, straddling the Polish-Soviet frontier, stretches the last substantial surviving remnant of the primeval woodland: the mixed deciduous and coniferous Bialowiecza Forest, parts of which have never been inter-fered with by man. It is one of the few areas in the world where the European bison roams wild, along with the elk, boar, deer, wolf, lynx and that rare denizen of the streams of forest meadows, the beaver. Whoever sees this forest sees Europe as it was thousands of years ago.

On the moist floor of an English woodland, a three-inch common shrew hastily consumes a worm before setting off in search of another meal. This agile, velvety creature must feed almost constantly to maintain the rapid metabolism of its tiny body: day and night it scurries about with an air of nervous agitation, feeding for three hours, resting for the next three and then feeding again.

For 500 years the Bialowiecza Forest was the private hunting domain of the kings of Poland and the tsars of Russia, who endowed it with special privileges, and prohibited wood clearing and exploitation. Royal protection enabled this remnant of European forest to survive into the 20th Century, but during the First World War that protection came to an end; and between 1915 and 1918 the forest was occupied by soldiers of the German army, who carried off five million cubic metres of wood for the war effort and exterminated a large part of the wildlife. Most of the damage was done in the first three months, when the bulk of the larger species were gunned down for soldiers' food. There had been 700 elk in Bialowiecza at the beginning of the war; at the end of it there were only three. Wild boar, which had numbered more than 2,300, were down to a few score. The red deer, an abundant animal of the chase, were reduced to six. And the bison, the largest animal of all, was reduced from 727 in August, 1915, to 120 by December of the same year, and the reduction in numbers continued as the war went on.

That devastation led influential scientists of the re-formed Polish nation to make a strong effort to save the forest. By 1932 the National Park of Bialowiecza had been established, and although foreign armies again occupied the forest during the Second World War, it did not suffer the same destruction it had experienced during the First World War. In 1947, following the division of the forest into two parts as a result of the new frontiers between Poland and the U.S.S.R., the Polish National Park of Bialowiecza was re-established and it is now an important centre for scientific forest research and bison studies.

In order to see this ancient forest with its unique herds of wild bison and rare colonies of beaver, I set out for Bialowiecza in the last days of September. My departure was precipitate, for the trees in England were already beginning to shed a few leaves and I did not want to find the primeval forest bare. I flew to Warsaw, hired a car and drove hurriedly north-eastwards across the flat Polish plains in the direction of the Soviet frontier. It was a day of high Indian summer, warm and blue, and the leaves of the aspen trees along the road were a brilliant yellow and flickered like coins. By the time I reached Hajnowka, at the western edges of the Bialowiecza Forest, it was dark.

The road into the forest was alive with frogs—a whole army of frogs crossing the road from right to left in a northerly direction, and jumping up and down in the beams of the car headlamps. The dark trees on either side of the road were of an immense height. I had never seen such big trees on this continent. They towered over me and crowded in on me, so that driving down the straight road between them was like driving through an endless tunnel. I continued for 11 miles before I came to the village of Bialowiecza in a clearing near the frontier. On the other side of that frontier the forest extended an additional six miles.

The entire Bialowiecza Forest is 486 square miles in area, of which 228 square miles lie in Poland and 258 square miles in the U.S.S.R. The forest grows on a slightly elevated, gently rolling plain from whose peat bogs flow numerous streams and rivers: the Lesna in the south, the Narew to the north, and its tributary the Narewka which flows 37 miles through the heart of the forest. Much of the Bialowiecza Forest is systematically and scientifically managed for its valuable timber, but between the Narewka and its tributary, the Hwozna, lies what is called "the strict reservation", where the forest is left to itself and where no one is allowed to set foot without special permission. This is the Bialowiecza National Park, 20 square miles of the forest, interspersed with marshes and meadows, where time has stood still—not for decades or even generations, but for millennia. It was this part of the forest I planned to explore.

The climate of Bialowiecza is Eastern European—that is to say, continental and extreme. There may be a difference over the year of up to 85°F between maximum and minimum temperatures, and in winter the thermometer may fall as low as −40°F (although −22°F to −25°F is normal) and the snow may cover the ground for three to five months. Winter is perhaps the most distinctive season in Bialowiecza. The snow is deep and clean and frozen; the evergreens are heavily burdened; and the boars and the wolves and the lynx range far and wide in their search for food. You travel by horse-sleigh in winter, hissing over the frosty snow behind clouds of steam from the horses' nostrils.

But early spring is a distinctive time, too. The wild flowers, of which there are 1,150 different species, bloom in great profusion all over the forest floor in that brief period when the sun can reach them while the trees are still bare. As soon as the trees put on their leaves, however, the canopy closes overhead, plunging the ground into shade, so that few plants are seen in flower thereafter.

On a warm morning early in October I finally set off on foot to the strict reservation of the Bialowiecza Forest. The approach lay along a track across a clearing of peasant smallholdings. Along this track the last tsars had clip-clopped their way to the day's hunt, with their retinue of foot followers, trackers, beaters, skinners, cooks and bearers, their boar-lances and rifles, their picnic hampers of vodka and venison. Ahead and to right and to left as far as the eye could see lay the edge of the primeval forest, and I was relieved to see that the leaves were still green on the trees.

Approaching the forest was like approaching the ramparts of some medieval walled town. The long line of trees ahead presented a high, sheer, solid front, silent except for the croaking of a dozen ravens wheeling about a group of tall hornbeam trees a little inside the forest. At the end of the track stood an immense gate, nearly three times the height of a man, constructed of vast beams pegged with large wooden rivets. I passed through this portcullis into the strict reservation. The trees shut out the human world like a door closing behind me, and I entered a natural world like none I had ever seen before.

I perceived this fact instantly. My eyes had to adjust to the gloom under the dense canopy of the trees. My skin registered the drop in temperature and the increase in humidity. (In summer, humidity inside the forest may reach 100 per cent.) My nose picked up the rank, dank vegetable odour of leaf mould, humus, bog water and decaying wood. In that silent place my ears registered every sound, so that even the minutest noise seemed magnified: a pine cone fell on the soft forest floor with a thud like a hammer blow, a maple leaf fluttered down among the branches with a clatter like broken crockery, the mad cackle of a jay and the rattle of a woodpecker echoed and re-echoed between the myriad noise-reflecting surfaces of the tree trunks like the uproar of a blasphemous congregation in a cathedral.

But it was on my innermost sense that the forest made the strongest impression. It seemed to me that in the Bialowiecza Forest one was confronted with a kind of mirror-image of the inner recesses of the human mind; and in the continuous cycle of growth, death, decay and regeneration that I saw all around, I was painfully reminded of our own mortality, and of the biochemical function we would each have to perform sooner or later when we gave back to the common pool the cells of which we, like all other living things, are composed.

There are various reasons why the Bialowiecza Forest makes such an extraordinary impact. First, the trees are overwhelmingly tall and of shapes few Europeans nowadays are accustomed to. The oaks are not the squat, spreading types we normally see: here they are giants soaring upwards more than 130 feet, with massive, dead-straight, branchless trunks surmounted by tiny round crowns of leaves. The spruces reach an unbelievable height of nearly 160 feet, the limes 130 feet, the ash

129 feet, the Scots pines 125 feet, the maples 120 feet, and the goat willows 72 feet. They are splendid trees.

Second—the mark of every true wilderness—signs of man are almost totally absent. In the Bialowiecza strict reservation nothing has been done to interfere with the natural rhythm of self-regeneration: no tree has been chopped down, no fallen trunk has been sawn up or carted off, no seed or sapling has been planted. What happens to the trees of the forest is their own business. As a consequence the forest looks like a cross between an arboreal boneyard and a nursery, with seedlings, saplings and young trees all competing for space and light in the gap left by a fallen giant.

Everywhere I saw the litter of death and destruction. Trees seemed to have met their end in as many ways as men reach theirs, dying as a result of old age, or accident, or even murder. I saw a huge Scots pine that had been split from crown to root by a single stroke of lightning as if it were a piece of firewood. The impact of that terrifying blow had not felled the tree, but it had thrown off gigantic chips of clean white wood up to 12 feet long; and although the branches high up in the canopy still spread their dark green needle leaves, the tree could not have long to live. In Bialowiecza, thunderbolts are so common and so dangerous that forest guards ask visitors to leave when a storm approaches; in the stormy month of January no visitors are allowed into the forest.

High winds, too, are a frequent cause of havoc. Many an ailing tree has been nudged to its death when the winter gales from the east shriek across the canopy; and when a tree falls, it drags down other living trees with it, or uproots them when their roots are entangled with its own. I frequently saw as many as five or six trees lying beside one another, all brought down together. Giant spruces lay sprawled over the forest floor, like the skeletons of stranded whales or the ribs and keel of some ancient wooden ship. Other trees still stood where they had died, disintegrating slowly, bit by bit.

The oldest tree in the forest was a Scots pine, nearly 110 feet high and with a trunk of massive girth. It was still just alive at the top, but all its lower branches were naked and dead. It had sprouted from a seed at about the time Sir Francis Drake sailed round the world; by the time Shakespeare had written *Hamlet* it was already a mature tree. Previously the oldest tree had been a 650-year-old oak; but not long ago it was struck by lightning and toppled to the ground. It still lay stretched over the ground, a noble carcass, its trunk wrapped in an inch-thick cover of green moss, like a pile carpet. The trunk had

In the Bialowiecza Forest, thick moss covers the trunk of a 650-year-old oak tree felled by lightning. The tree's death is part of the continuing cycle of decomposition and growth: the trunk has already begun to disintegrate under the attack of fungi and wood-boring insects, while a tiny oak sapling has begun to sprout from its side.

already decayed sufficiently to support a variety of plant life, including a small oak sapling, which conceivably was growing out of the very tree that spawned it as an acorn.

It takes ten to 20 years for a dead tree to complete the next stage of the forest cycle of life and death, to rot into humus and return to the ground from which it came. All over the forest floor at Bialowiecza I saw trees in every stage of decay and transfiguration. Many were in an intermediate state. Their roots and lower trunk remained whole, but the top of the trunk had dissolved and melted into the soil, while the middle, a fertile patch for grubs and fungi of all kinds, was so soft you could push your hand through it.

Never have I seen such a wealth of fungi as I encountered on my first excursion into the Bialowiecza Forest. Altogether there are 900 different species. I saw bright, sticky, yellow mushrooms like Swiss confectionery (*Pholiota aurivella*); fungi with little water beads hanging down from their parasols (*Lepiota rhacodes*); fungi like white candy floss (*Hiericium coralloides*); and bracket mushrooms like underwater scallops. A fallen hornbeam was covered from root to crown in a quilt of yellowish-orange fungi of an edible species called honey mushroom (*Armillaria mellea*), which is delicious roasted. The dead trunk, perhaps a hundred feet long and five feet in diameter at the base, was wrapped so thickly in fungi that barely an inch of its surface was visible.

A beam of sunlight shone through a small gap in the forest canopy overhead and in this beam I could see a powdery haze given off by the tree. At first I thought it was a cloud of mushroom spores; then I realized that the tree was steaming as it rotted. The mushrooms, too, would rot in a few days and turn brown and slimy. Every living thing was locked into this cycle of death and metamorphosis.

The Bialowiecza Forest contains many habitats. Within the strict reservation alone there is peat bog, marsh, meadow, river and a bewildering permutation of tree stands which defy satisfactory classification. What kind of tree grows where in the forest, and in association with what other kinds of trees, depends on the nature of the soil, which in turn depends partly on the water balance. In the river valleys and on lower ground the soil varies from mud-marshy to marshy-peat to peat. Between the rivers, in the eastern part of the strict reservation, it consists of slightly loamy sand. In the south-west, on the borders of the Bialowiecza village clearing, the soil is clay or sand on clay.

The deciduous trees thrive on damp and fertile soils, the evergreens on dry and sandy ones. Altogether 26 species of tree are found in the forest, of which the dominant variety is the hornbeam, which forms a distinct community in 35 per cent of the primeval forest and shares a further 10 per cent with oak. The other distinct communities are alder and pine, and to a lesser extent spruce, oak and ash. Thirty-seven per cent of the trees are more than a hundred years old.

To see all the different habitats on foot would have been an arduous and time-consuming business. My next excursion into the strict reservation, therefore, was by horse and cart—the traditional V-shaped Polish country cart, like a dug-out canoe on wheels. Accompanying me on the journey was the head of the excellent Bialowieczka National Park museum, Dr. Czeslaw Okolow. A tall, bearded, amiable and most erudite man, with a great passion for nature and wild places and an amazing memory, Dr. Okolow knew the names of every bird, insect and flower in the forest, not just in Polish and Latin, but in English, French, German and Russian as well. I learned a great deal from him that day.

It was not only an informative day, it was a most idyllic one. A horse and cart is a most unfairly neglected means of travel; this cart had pneumatic rubber tyres which made no noise, so that the only sound we could hear was the soft clop of hoofs on the lonely forest floor, and we glided gently beneath the trees like a boat down a smooth river. This way and that we peered, up and down, backwards and forwards. The primeval forest—a rotting, steaming, cool, green vegetable world— swallowed us up and we travelled back in time to an age before civilization. It was like voyaging along the bottom of some mysterious ocean.

There was no clearer indication of the different zones of the forest than our own changes of mood. When we entered a deciduous zone—of hornbeam perhaps, or oak and birch—our spirits rose and we chatted and laughed and looked around, for the deciduous forest seemed bright and green and alive. But whenever we came to a coniferous zone of pine and spruce, our spirits appeared to sink; we became silent and introspective and stared fixedly ahead, for by comparison the coniferous forest seemed dark and gloomy and lifeless.

Not that the forest was in any way lifeless. The observant, polyglot Dr. Okolow never missed a species of plant or fungus or bird if it was visible from the track and never failed to point it out to me as we jogged by in our cart. "*Picea excelsa!*" he declared, waving his hand towards a particularly tall spruce. "*Tilia cordata! Pholiota aurivella!* Not edible, I think. What we call *luswiak zlotawy!* Champignons, you might say." He pointed suddenly to a black and white bird half-way up an old hornbeam tree. "Look! There, you see? In that *Carpinus betulus* —a *Dendrocopus medius*, a *Mittelspecht*, how do you call it, *pic mar*? A middle spotted woodpecker, that's it! In Russian it is . . . what is it in Russian? *Sredny poistry datel*. Yes."

It was not easy to observe the birds and animals in the forest: the trees were too dense, the wild creatures too shy and elusive, the horse and cart too obvious. Once I spotted a red squirrel foraging along the side of the track. Later I smelt the pungent musty odour of wild boar in a boggy patch of ground among some alders. From time to time I heard a stag roaring eerily among the trees. At the western edge of the strict reservation—in the swampy meadows of the Narewka, where small pioneer birches and stunted willows were slowly converting swamp into forest, as they had done elsewhere at the end of the Ice Age—I saw jays and wild duck and a short-toed eagle crossing the clearing. But otherwise Bialowiecza's wildlife was not immediately in evidence.

And yet, as Dr. Okolow meticulously explained to me, the fauna of Bialowiecza is exceptionally rich and in the Polish part of the forest there are 11,000 different species of animals: 8,500, he explained, were insect species (the insect world of Bialowiecza has no equal in Central Europe); 206 were species of spiders; 24, fish; and 227, birds (48 resident)—including black storks and cranes, eagles, eagle owls, great grey owls and pigmy owls, kites, ruffs, black grouse, capercaillie, rollers, hoopoes, crossbills and ortolans. Among the mammals, the smaller species included hedgehogs, moles, voles and shrews; 13 species of bat; 19 species of rodent; foxes, badgers, otters, racoon dogs, pine martens, polecats and brown hare. There are no longer any wild cats or wolverines; and the last brown bear was seen in 1963, when a single individual walked in from the Soviet side, stayed for two weeks, didn't like it, and walked back across the border. But according to the 1980 Polish census there was still a fair population of larger mammals, including 1,100 red deer, 900 roe deer, 930 boar, 35 elk, 15 lynx, 4 wolves and—*pièce de résistance*—more than 304 bison.

The story of the European bison's return from extinction and its restitution in a wild state at Bialowiecza is a remarkable one. In the past the animal was common throughout Europe as far north as southern Sweden and as far east as Siberia. But unlike its relative, the bison or buffalo of the North American plains, the European bison is essentially a forest animal; and, with the gradual destruction of the European forests, it was forced farther and farther eastwards. In England it was exterminated in the 8th Century, in Sweden in the 11th, in France in the 14th, in eastern Germany in the 18th. By 1914 the entire population of wild bison in Europe was confined to two natural outposts: Bialowiecza (where the lowland forest species lived) and the Caucasus (where the mountain forest species lived).

In the hungry months following the withdrawal of the German army from Bialowiecza at the end of the First World War, the few remaining free bison were slaughtered, the last one falling to a poacher at the end of March or the beginning of April, 1919. In 1927 the last free bison in the Caucasus was shot, a victim of the turmoil following the Russian Revolution. Thereafter the only European bison were 54 zoo specimens. But in 1923, a group of conservationists had met at the Berlin Zoo and formed the International Association for the Preservation of the European Bison, with the object of breeding bison in captivity.

In 1929 preparatory work was begun on the restitution of bison in Poland. Two cows were brought to Bialowiecza from a zoo in Sweden to join a Polish bull called Plisch—and from them stem all the members of the present herd. By 1939 their number had grown to 16. The Second World War left the herd relatively unharmed. The Nazis killed a few until Hermann Goering, who expected that one day the Bialowiecza Forest would be his own private hunting estate, issued a decree protecting the bison. By the end of the war there were still 16 bison and they have increased in number ever since. By 1978, in addition to the bison in the Polish part of the forest, there were more than a hundred on the Soviet side, and about 2,000 world-wide—including zoo specimens. Luckily bison breed well in captivity and the species can be considered to be out of immediate danger.

I saw my first wild bison at half-past five in the morning, when I had been out of bed only ten minutes. It was a lone bull, a huge creature standing quietly in a pool of pale sunlight at the edge of a clearing. It was as high as me, six feet or more, and must have weighed nearly a ton. Its coat was chestnut-brown, and very thick and shaggy along the back of its head, chest and nape: its neck was short, high and incredibly powerful looking, with a dewlap that reached to its chest; and its curved horns spread upwards, outwards and forwards. These animals are as strong as they look. Some time ago one of them was involved in a collision with a car, albeit a small, light model, and the impact left the bull standing but the car a wreck at the side of the road. They can also run at 40 miles an hour through forest thickets, jump over a six-foot fence, and crash through all but the heftiest barriers.

A European bison bull, part of the only wild herd in existence today, roams through the undergrowth of Poland's Bialowiecza Forest.

Clearly, looking for a herd in the forest required some degree of caution. Equally clearly, looking for wild animals in a forest nearly twice the size of the Isle of Wight required some degree of luck as well. I was fortunate in having the Bison Master of the Bialowiecza National Park with me that morning. Wlodzimierz Piroznikov, a wartime Spitfire pilot, and a most obliging guide, had been responsible for the welfare and breeding of the Bialowiecza bison for several years and he knew the most likely place to look for them. As forest creatures, bison prefer to live in the shade under the canopy. Normally they come out into the clearings only in the early morning and late evening, when they are most active in their search for food: herbs, shrubs, saplings, soft bark. This was the reason for our early start.

At about 7 o'clock, in the broad green meadow of the Lutownia, a tributary stream of the Narewka, we came across the first herd. There were about 30 bison—cows and calves—mostly lying down in the gentle morning sunshine, or rolling on their backs and waving their legs in the air like lambs. The bulls had by now left the females, for they join them only in the mating season during August and September; during the rest of the year they roam independently, either in bull herds or alone. Old bulls, like the one I had encountered first thing that morning, often never rejoin the herds. They concede leadership of the females to the younger males and withdraw from communal life, spending the remainder of their lives in solitude.

For a while, we watched the herd through field glasses; but when we tried to get nearer, the animals rose to their feet and stood watching us with an air of docile caution. When we approached a little closer, they slowly turned and with a leisurely amble began to head for the dark cover of the forest on the far side of the meadow, their outlines foggy from the steam that rose from their bodies. One by one they silently vanished into the deep shade of the trees. It was as though they had momentarily stepped out of history, and then stepped back in again.

A little later, not far from the first herd, I spotted more bison through the trees. This time, under the cover of the forest, we were able to stalk up to within a few yards of them. There were about a dozen animals browsing at the edge of a clearing, all cows and calves. They peered cautiously at us as I ducked and weaved among the trees to get a better shot with my camera before they fled. Photography under such circumstances concentrates the mind wonderfully. Only when the bison finally lost patience with my antics and galloped off as nimbly as young stags did it occur to me that I could have been hurt.

The tell-tale scalloped markings of a beaver's incisors ring the trunk of a mature black alder near the Hwozna River in the Bialowiecza Forest. Once the tree has been felled to make a dam, the beaver will strip off its bark and also the cambium—the tender sap-carrying layer just under its bark—for food.

"Normally," Mr. Piroznikov explained afterwards, "you should carry a large square of red or white cloth and, if the bison comes towards you, you should flash the cloth in front of you. If that doesn't stop the bison, then you should climb a tree. And if you can't do that, you should walk backwards very slowly and be careful never to turn your back on the bison. One of my men broke the rule and turned round. He was gored in the lower back and his thigh bone was broken. He is still too ill to work.

"Of course they can be dangerous. They are wild animals and they weigh nearly a ton. A herd can suddenly surround you and start closing in on you. Even if they are only curious, you can get badly crushed and mauled. They have never been domesticated by man—they are too unpredictable. The Moscow State Circus asked us for two, but they gave up trying to train them because they never knew what the bison were thinking. Anyway, bison don't like being touched. You should never touch a bison, they're very sensitive about that."

The bison of Bialowiecza are not totally independent of man. In winter, when they gather into larger herds of 80 or a hundred, they are provided with beetroot and hay at nine feeding places throughout the forest. This is partly to ensure they do not starve, partly to stop them destroying the forest by stripping bark off too many trees: left to its own devices each bison would need 100 acres of forest to sustain it. Three reservations at Bialowiecza have been set aside for captive bison, which are kept for pedigree breeding and export to zoos in Poland and abroad. thirty bison are always kept in enclosures as a reserve against epidemics or some other catastrophe that could lay waste the free herds.

Of all the wild animals of Europe, my favourites are the wolf and the beaver: the wolf because to me it symbolizes the call of the wilds; the beaver because, as a boy, I was brought up on *Pilgrims of the Wild* and other books by Grey Owl, a man who befriended this endearing but persecuted creature. I knew that my chances of seeing a wolf at Bialowiecza were extremely slight. (As it turned out I was right.) But I had greater hopes of seeing something of beavers, if only because they leave substantial traces of their presence in the form of the dams they build across streams. Beavers have long been hunted for their valuable fur and medicinal musk, and in Bialowiecza they became extinct half a century before the bison. But in 1956, they were reintroduced into the Soviet part of the forest, and later that year one of the families immigrated from the Soviet side and settled along the Hwozna River, which forms the northern boundary of the Bialowiecza National Park. In spite of occasional poaching—punished by a severe fine—the original beaver family has now become three, and it was these three families that I set out to find, accompanied by Dr. Okolow.

It was a warm, cloudless morning and the wide strip of reed-filled meadow along the Hwozna was very beautiful and peaceful. On either side stood the sharp, sheer edge of the forest, the tall hornbeams and oaks yellowing a little with the onset of autumn. The narrow, shallow ribbon of the river ran clear and gently over its bed of deep, soft, sandy silt. Big blue and yellow-striped dragon-flies flickered above the surface of the water. Ahead of us came the sudden, urgent clatter of wings and the cry of mallards flying out of sight behind the high reeds and grasses. Dr. Okolow and I walked east along a muddy game trail leading to the Soviet border. The footmarks of wild boar and elk were imprinted in the black boggy ground, and I saw deer droppings and a spot where the bank had been dug up by boar looking for roots and grubs.

There was no mistaking the first beaver dam when we got to it. It was like a building site where the workers had downed tools. A black alder on the river bank had been chewed into the shape of an egg-timer. The bite marks of the beaver's two big front incisors were clearly visible all over the cut surface of the tree trunk, as if it had been hewn with a small adze. A beaver, I was told, can nibble through a three-inch tree trunk in five minutes, and through quite a thick one in an hour. But it cannot always control the direction of the fall, and sometimes the beaver is killed when the tree crashes on top of it.

The tree I saw on the Hwozna that morning would not have fallen across the stream, because another standing tree would have obstructed its descent. But the beaver had previously succeeded in dropping a different tree across the river, and it now formed the basis of a half-finished dam. The downstream side of the tree was interlaced with twigs and branches. In time, leaves and logs and other debris brought down by the stream would be caught in the barrier, silt would build up against it, seeds would fall and sprout on it, and before long it would be a solid dam on which a man could walk.

A quarter of a mile farther up the stream we found a second dam that had reached this stage. It was about 30 feet long and overgrown with rank vegetation. On the far side the beavers had created a sluice. By controlling the size of the sluice they could control the level of the river behind the dam. The river was very low because of a dry summer following an abnormal winter, during which it snowed for one month instead of the usual four. The beavers had therefore closed the sluice so that the water was four feet deeper above the dam than below it.

There was a third dam, Dr. Okolow told me, by the Soviet border half a mile away, but there would be little point in going there. We were unlikely actually to see any beavers, for they are wary, nocturnal creatures. We therefore turned our steps westwards. On the way back we took a short cut through the forest and the ticks in the trees fell down on us by the score. I buttoned up my shirt collar to keep them out, but I still had two with me when I arrived in Warsaw late that night.

It was odd, I thought then, that these creatures should still be active this late in the year—perhaps it was because of the warm weather prolonged so far into autumn. But the next morning a freezing wind was blowing off the Vistula and the people walked the streets of Warsaw with their collars turned up, huddled against the chill. Winter was coming, and soon a deep blanket of snow would settle over the great primeval forest I had left behind at Bialowiecza.

Plants of the Shadows

In the shadowy world of Europe's deciduous woods, where often only meagre sunlight dips through the canopied treetops, many of the plants that have the greatest chance of survival are parasites and saprophytes. Unlike green plants, which use the energy their chlorophyll absorbs from the sunlight to manufacture food for themselves, these plants flourishing in the gloom draw their nutriments directly from other organisms—living or dead.

Common among the forest parasites—those plants that feed on other live plants—are the delicate purple toothwort and the pinkish-white dodder. The toothwort thrives on beech, poplar and hazel tree roots that have grown close to the surface, and the ubiquitous dodder coils its slender red stems firmly around nettles, whinbushes, hops or other plants, penetrating the hosts with its many tiny suckers.

A large number of woodland fungi are also parasites, preying on plants and trees. Others, however, are saprophytes, or scavengers, surviving on dead organic matter, and these have a vital dual role to play in the life of the forest. They are important agents in the decomposition of woodland litter—the regular accumulation of plant and animal residues—and its conversion into humus. Some also grow in mutually beneficial association with trees, including oak, beech and hornbeam, and with flowering plants, especially terrestrial orchids.

In this association, which is known as mycorrhizal, the fungus either grows round the outside of its partner's roots or else penetrates their internal tissues, and each plant provides nourishment for the other. In the forests, the mycorrhizal partnership is widespread, and for some plants it is essential to survival.

The minute seeds of orchids are unable to germinate unless they form a relationship with a mycorrhizal fungus. Having made the right contact, the seedlings grow saprophytically, drawing on vital carbon compounds accumulated by the fungus. Some species of orchid, such as the bird's nest, and other plants including the yellow bird's nest, remain wholly saprophytic even after successful germination. The fungal association also persists throughout the life of green-leaved orchids, which is odd, because after germination the orchids can synthesize their own food. The significance of this lifelong partnership is a mystery.

The purple toothwort (right), its clusters of bright flowers clenched like a claw, has the descriptive Latin name, Lathraea clandestina. Lacking chlorophyll, it feeds off the roots of various deciduous trees and can be found radiating in lines from the bases of tree trunks, following the paths of roots lying just below the surface.

Taking its name from its pouch-shaped lower petal, the lady's slipper orchid (left) is green-leaved and is thus able to absorb and utilize sunlight to produce its own food. But as a seedling its survival depends on the presence of a fungal partner to provide it with nourishment. The partnership continues even after the orchid has matured.

The elegant lady orchid (right), which flowers between April and June, thrives in the shadowy woodlands of Europe and grows from one to two feet high. Like the lady's slipper orchid, it is green-leaved and capable of synthesizing the food that it needs, but will not germinate unless it makes contact with a mycorrhizal fungus.

The yellow bird's nest (left), a perennial of the Wintergreen family, emerges from beneath its quilt of decaying leaves. Found in beech woods, it is a saprophyte and blooms between June and September. Its waxy-looking stem bears scaly, yellow-brown leaves that indicate its lack of chlorophyll.

The sallow-flowered, brown-stemmed bird's nest orchid (right) lives off the nutrients processed by its fungal partner from beechwood humus. This sweet-smelling plant, up to a foot high, derives its name from its mass of underground roots, which have the tangled appearance of a bird's nest.

Nourished during its development by decaying organic matter, the shaggy ink cap mushroom (above) has just discharged its millions of spores. But having spawned new life, the mushroom itself will soon die, its gill tissues liquefying and dripping away like ink.

Pelted by rain, the puffball fungi (right) have released their spores for dispersal and now lie sagging against one another. One puffball has just been collapsed by a rain drop and the cloud of spores it has ejected lingers before being swept away by the wind.

5/ The Deserts of Andalucia

Après nous, le désert.   GRAFFITI ON A WALL IN PARIS, MAY, 1968

The three peninsulas of southern Europe abutting the Mediterranean Sea—the Iberian Peninsula, the Balkan Peninsula and the long arm of Italy—contain the drylands of the continent, with their barren plains, their scrubby hills, their hot semi-deserts, their celebrated blue Mediterranean skies. They are widely different regions, with different histories, different cultures and different landforms. But they all have one characteristic in common: they are all a Paradise Lost, a ravaged Eden.

The face of the Mediterranean world has been ruined by man. The classical civilizations of Greece and Rome largely destroyed their natural landscapes; the medieval kingdoms of Spain and Portugal did the same. Nowadays the most eroded parts of southern Europe are true wilderness areas, virtually uninhabited and hostile to man. Only in a few places— along parts of the shores, high in the mountains and in some of the river deltas—do pockets of the primeval landscape survive intact. Among them, though, are some of the largest and most important wildlife sanctuaries in the continent, remnants of a fertile past.

Three thousand years ago the Mediterranean hinterland was a very green and pleasant world, with a luxuriant forest cover and a rich fauna to match. In those halcyon days the forest stretched from the Atlantic coast of Iberia to the Mediterranean coast of Asia, and reached from the shore-line to the hills. For the most part it was an open canopy woodland with dense undergrowth in which the holm or evergreen oak, with its splendid crown of foliage, was the predominant tree. But on the sandy soils grew cedars and cypresses and stone pines, and on the mountains there were dense forests of montane conifers which reached up to the timber line.

Looking now at the ruined landscapes of Andalucia or Calabria or Parnassus, it is difficult to believe that they were once the sites of a full-blown, climax forest, where Mediterranean lions roared at sundown and the fallow deer roamed in large herds. Where the Parthenon now stands on the barren hills above Athens, there once was a forest of oak and pine. Where Cannes sprawls amid dry rocks at the foot of the maritime Alps, there was a wilderness of evergreen oaks and laurels.

All this disappeared through a simple cycle of degeneration. The trees of the forest were cut down to clear ground for crops and grazing, and to provide timber for charcoal, fires, ships and buildings. With the forest cover gone, the soil was exposed to the ravages of erosion. The rainwaters ran swiftly down the hills, taking the top soil with them, and year after year the ground grew stonier and stonier. As long ago as 360 B.C. the Greek philosopher Plato noticed the effects of this process on his native country. In his *Critias* he wrote: "The soil in the highlands is constantly eroding away; it keeps sliding ceaselessly and disappearing into the sea. Compared with what it was formerly like, there now remains only, so to speak, the bones of a body emaciated by an illness: the soft rich soil has been washed away, and only the skeleton of the land remains. There are some mountains here which have nothing but food for bees, though they had trees not so long ago."

The effects of erosion were made worse by herds of domestic goats—after man, the single most destructive animal in the Mediterranean. The goats browsed upon young trees and saplings before they could grow to any size, the forest passed beyond any possibility of natural regeneration and gave way to the classic vegetation cover of uncultivated Mediterranean lands today: the *maquis*. The *maquis* is a tangled scrub of thorny creepers, stunted oaks, strawberry trees, myrtles and wild olives—thickets of low, prickly vegetation that are often impenetrable. The *maquis* is not the ultimate stage of degeneration. Where bush fires sweep through it during the hot dry summers it degenerates even further into *garrigue*, a sparse growth of cistus shrubs or aromatic thyme, rosemary and lavender, kermes oaks and dwarf palms—vegetation adapted to near-desert conditions. After the *garrigue* there is only desert.

No European country has suffered so much from erosion as Spain. Flying over the high tableland that makes up most of that country, one might be forgiven for supposing that it was chiefly desert land, and indeed many large areas now are semi-deserts where only a wandering shepherd or huntsman relieves the monotony of the vast horizon. It is probably true to say that Spain is the wildest country in Europe south of the Arctic Circle—and not only for the endless, ruined steppes of her central tableland. There are still bears in Spain, and wolves, mongooses, lammergeiers, great bustards—and snakes and lizards everywhere.

During a journey I made into Spain I focused my attention on the most southerly parts of the country where the landscape and wildlife of Europe closely resemble North Africa's. I aimed to see wilderness areas both man-made and natural, and not only drylands but (as I will relate in the next chapter) wetlands as well. My chief intention was to reach the incomparable delta of the River Guadalquivir in the Gulf of Cadiz, where I would be able to explore the desert sands and scrubland of the Coto Doñana nature reserve and then venture into the great primeval expanse of Las Marismas, one of the largest and most important marshlands remaining in Europe. But first I made a point of visiting the province of Almeria in the south-east corner of Spain, a region more barren and eroded than any other place in the continent.

Northwards from the Cabo de Gata on the coast, across the plain of the Campo de Nijar to the southern foothills of the Sierra de los Filabres, the countryside is arid in the extreme, and in the region west of the township of Tabernas it is reduced to its elemental substructure of Miocene clay. No other part of Spain, no other part of the most desiccated and misused regions of Greece or southern Italy can approach the Tabernas badlands for sheer physical destruction. In large part this destruction, as elsewhere in the Mediterranean, is the consequence of man's improvidence; but it is also the result of nature's inclemency. The Tabernas area lies in the rain shadow of the Sierra Nevada, and the south-westerly winds are empty of moisture by the time they have crossed the mountains. An average of only four and a half inches of rain fall on·Tabernas each year —less than the average for the driest part of the Australian desert—and midsummer temperatures may reach 110° F. Such rain as does fall may come in a sudden storm lasting a few hours, when the water runs rapidly off the hills and rushes down the valleys in devastating flash-floods that erode the landscape still further.

I was exploring wild Europe at a time when normal weather patterns were disturbed. I had had to endure unprecedented heavy snow in the Alps in late spring. At Bialowiecza I had found autumn much prolonged,

The brilliant blossoms of Cytinus hypocistus nestle amid the leaf-and-twig litter of Mediterranean scrubland. Because the plant has fleshy orange scales instead of green leaves, and thus lacks chlorophyll with which to manufacture nutrients, it survives as a parasite, hijacking nourishment from the spreading roots of other dryland plants such as the cistus shrub.

and when I reached the Tabernas badlands early one summer morning, it rained. It did not rain much, it is true—but it rained. Where there should have been an incandescent white sky of almost Saharan vindictiveness, there were big, blue-grey rain clouds that reminded me of Hastings on a wet Bank Holiday. Finding a vantage point from which I could see five or six miles, I looked out across a terrain of hills and deep gullies stretching to the distant mountains. It was a stark, grey-coloured world unrelieved by a single tree, a landscape of mud that resembled the dried remains of a front-line trench system from the Western Front. "*Muy salvaje paisaje*," said the local Spaniards. "Very wild country."

And yet, as I found when I entered a maze of deeply eroded gullies that led into the interior of this waste, there was a surprising amount of life. Oleander bushes with brilliant pink flowers and stands of dazzling yellow Spanish broom grew in the gully-beds. Rabbits skittered for cover among the rocks, martins swooped overhead, a crested lark managed a half song, a few semi-quavers of monody dribbling from its half-open beak. A stagnant yellow puddle was alive with black, jack-knifing mosquito larvae and rimmed with dead and dying bees that had drunk the water and been poisoned by the high concentration of soluble salts sucked out of the ground by capillary action.

At the bottom of one of the gullies the ground was covered with a thick salty crust, and to walk on it was like walking on crisp frozen snow. Elsewhere the surface was drier and cracked into pieces of crazy paving the size and convexity of old sandwiches. Withered bushes with brittle twigs and snatching thorns sent tap-roots 15 feet long snaking over the arid ground like hosepipes looking for water. A litter of dried bric-a-brac lay scattered about: dead palm leaves, segments of dead palm trunks, pieces of bleached wood brought down by some sudden flood. I was reminded exactly of similar places I had seen in Arabia and North Africa; even the smell, the unmistakable, musky, sweet smell of animal droppings and dust and decay was the same.

The gully descended steadily into the heart of the badlands. Three dead foxes lay in my path. They had been dead for some weeks, for they were as dry as cured skins. One, a large specimen and almost perfectly preserved, lay on its side like a dog asleep in front of a fire. There was nothing to indicate how it had died. If a huntsman had shot it, there was no sign of a bullet wound. Perhaps it had died of hunger. The bodies of the other two animals had been disturbed. The head of one lay at the foot of the cliff, its teeth bared in death in a frozen snarl; its legs lay entangled in the ransacked corpse of a third fox, as though they had died together in a moment of mutual violence. What drama had happened here I could only guess. But I was saddened that in a place so hostile to life, three members of the largest animal species living there should have met with simultaneous extinction.

By mid-morning the clouds had blown away and the sun beat down. In the enclosed space of the gully the air soon became stifling and I had become very thirsty by the time I saw signs of human habitation. A village of very old and curiously ramshackle wooden houses lay ahead. I thought of a bar, and cool beer, and clinking ice. I strode into the village, past a gallows with a rope noose hanging from it, and a crowded graveyard near by. The village looked deserted, as though its wells had dried up. The windows were broken, the planks of the wooden sidewalk were torn loose. I walked up to the swing doors of the saloon of the oddly named Western Union Hotel—and in a trice stepped through them, back into the desert landscape on the other side. The hotel had only two dimensions. It was a sham. The whole village was a sham—a film set put together out of lath and plaster for an old Western movie. So hostile was this desert of Almeria, this endless series of grey hills and ragged sierras, that even human influence had dwindled to something barely more substantial than a mirage.

A few days after my excursion into the eroded wastes of Tabernas I set off westwards to the Coto Doñana and Las Marismas in the delta of the Guadalquivir, the only Spanish river with a large coastal plain. My route took me from the Mediterranean to the Atlantic coast of Spain, and from a largely man-made wilderness to one that has so far largely escaped human interference.

The coast of the Gulf of Cadiz between Huelva and Sanlúcar de Barrameda, recently renamed the Costa de Luz or Coast of Light, is one of the most desert shores of Spain. For 38 miles, between the mouths of the Rio Tinto and the Guadalquivir, the straight, smooth beach of the Playa de Castilla is backed by a continuous range of gigantic sand dunes up to nine miles wide—the Arenas Gordas, the highest and broadest in Europe and equal in area to all the dunes of the 6,000-mile coast of Britain put together. These dunes are built of centuries' loads of sediment carried down from the sierras by the Guadalquivir and its tributaries, and thrown back on the shore by the combined forces of a prevailing Atlantic wind and a strong coastal current. The same geological process is in action now, and some of the dunes are advancing inland at the rate of 30 feet a year.

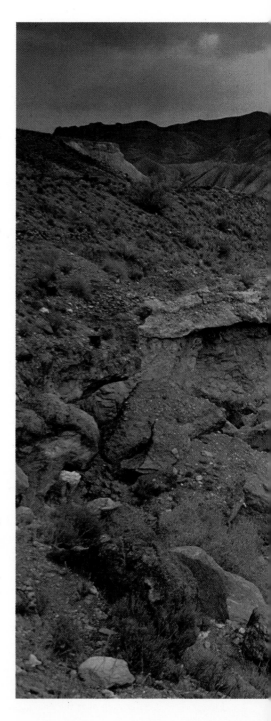

June storm clouds sweep over the unseasonably green desert of Almeria in southern Spain, muting the pink oleanders in an eroded gully.

Behind the Arenas Gordas lie 60 square miles of undisturbed heathland and stone pine woods where the vegetation has stabilized the sand. This wild stretch of country is the Coto Doñana. A former hunting ground for the dukes of Medina Sidonia, it was purchased with help from the World Wildlife Fund and is now a nature reserve. Farther inland again is the vast, flat expanse of Las Marismas, more than 500 square miles of marshland, largely dry and cracked in midsummer, flooded by rains and high tides during the rest of the year.

Together the Coto Doñana and Las Marismas contain a unique complex of habitats, and their fauna is as diverse as any in Europe. In a good year one-third of the bird species of the continent will come here, either to rest and feed during their migrations to and from Africa, or else to breed or pass the winter. Two of Europe's rarest creatures, the Spanish lynx and the Spanish imperial eagle, have one of their last strongholds here, and nowhere else in Europe is there a larger population of birds of prey—an indication of the wealth of small animal life.

I planned to devote the first part of my exploration to the drylands of the Coto Doñana and decided to start from the sea, walking across the desert dunes and working my way inland through zones increasingly rich in wildlife until I came to the Palacio de Doñana, once a hunting lodge and now the headquarters of the reserve's scientific station. There I would spend the night before venturing on horseback into the marshes of Las Marismas.

There was no one on the beach when I arrived there for the start of my journey—nobody, nothing. Along the coast of the Gulf of Cadiz, I could see perhaps five miles in either direction, and whichever way I looked I saw not a single soul, not one villa or beach bar or parasol. The shore was as wild and virgin as on the day of its creation.

The sun beat down out of a clear blue sky; the fine, dry, white sand burnt through the delicate soles of my city feet, so that I was compelled to hop from one to the other. On impulse, I took off my clothes and hung them on a withered, salty thorn bush, out of reach of ants and sand-hoppers; they fluttered in the sea wind like the tattered remnants of a nomad encampment.

I was seized with a spirit of bravura that afternoon—the solitude of that wilderness on the edge of the great ocean had this effect on me, as if I had reverted in a second to some earlier, archaic self. I ran into the sea and struck out manfully towards the continent of Africa. After a quarter of a mile, I turned and floated on my back; my body rose and

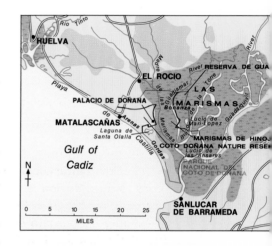

The Guadalquivir River Delta (above) covers 740 square miles of southern Spain. Along the Atlantic coast lie the dunes and scrubland encompassed by the Coto Doñana nature reserve; inland are the vast, bird-thronged marshes of Las Marismas. This unique wilderness area, partly zoned as a national park (red line), harbours as many animal species as any other place in Europe.

fell with the ocean swell, and from the crest of each wave, above the half moon of my ten white toes, I could catch a brief, shipwrecked sailor's view of the southern rim of Europe, before it sank from sight in the hollow of a wave and I could see nothing but the burning sky.

To my left, the dunes stretched away for mile after mile, whole cliffs and headlands of white and yellow sand that were finally lost in a mist of salt spray. These dunes were stationary, stabilized by plants; at El Asperillo, just north of the Coto boundary, they reached a height of 340 feet, the greatest altitude of any sand ridge in Europe, exceeding even the dunes of the Baltic coast of Poland. To my right stretched the shifting dunes, a vast region of windblown sand nine miles deep, steadily advancing inland grain by grain and wave by wave, 30 feet a year, overwhelming heaths and engulfing woods as they moved. The hazy outline of the headland at Sanlúcar de Barrameda marked the limits of this expansive desert vista.

I swam to the beach, dressed and headed inland. I climbed up the marram-covered fore-dunes, which at this point reached no more than 70 feet, and breasted the top in every expectation of a panoramic view over the Coto Doñana. But I was disappointed. Ahead of me stretched a fierce, white waste devoid of tracks and vegetation. Sterile, harsh, it dazzled me like a searchlight and scorched me like a fan-heater. A strong wind blew off the sea and bore the grains of fine white sand in a constant, fast-flowing stream towards the interior. The sand-stream covered the surface of the dunes with billions of airborne particles, like a fog; this fog, three inches high, gave the dunes a shimmering, dream-like quality and filled my footprints as quickly as an incoming tide on a beach. Nothing lived in this desolate solitude—no plant, no insect, no bird; the only things that moved were the wind and the sand, which resculpted the dunes from month to month and from year to year, so that nothing stayed constant and everything flowed.

In front of me, however, I knew there lay a whole sequence of habitats, one behind the other, reaching north-east through the Coto Doñana to the edges of Las Marismas. After the first line of dunes, I would pass through the following zones: the *corrales*, or woods of stone pines in the moist hollows on the landward side of the dunes; a line of seven freshwater lagoons running parallel with the coast at the back of the dune region; the treeless, sandy heathland of Halimium bushes (the most typical plant of the Coto, related to the cistus family, growing in thickets forming a low canopy under which small animals can find refuge); the cork oak savannah, park-like country where the

BEE ORCHID—OPHRYS APIFERA

Orchids and Orchid Lovers

To the casual observer, the bee and fly orchids of the open woods and sunny grasslands of the Mediterranean may look very much like the insects after which they are named. To the male insects drawn to them by an alluring scent the deception is apparently complete. So closely do the orchids' colours, shapes and scents resemble those of the female insects that the males actually attempt to copulate with the blossoms.

Everything about the flowers seems to have evolved towards this end. In each species, one of the petals has expanded into a fuzzy protruberance, or lip, at the back of which lie the flower's sexual organs, clustered together in a pollen-bearing column. When a male insect alights on the petal, it brushes against this column and picks up pollen, usually on its head and abdomen. Moving on to another orchid of the same species, it is quite likely to come into contact with such a column again, and some of the pollen on its body may be transferred. If cross-pollination occurs, the orchid will be fertilized.

FLY ORCHID—OPHRYS INSECTIFERA

tree cover becomes denser towards the east; and finally the no-man's land of seasonal marsh between dryland and wetland, stretching along a front some 19 miles long at the edge of Las Marismas.

I shuffled through the powdery, soft sand on the leeward sides of the dunes and tacked up the windward sides like a mountaineer on firm snow, for here the wind had compacted the sand into a harder, corrugated surface. After a while I came to a hollow, or *corral*, that had been overwhelmed by the sands. Scattered here and there, 50 yards apart, was all that remained of a stone pine copse that had flourished some years before: half a dozen excoriated tree trunks, their branches and upper stems sheared off about three feet above the ground, standing like fence posts and ringed by a scatter of broken old pine cones that marked the spot where the trees had once lived.

Soon I came to *corrales* at an intermediate stage of destruction. Here the stone pines had been engulfed more recently; although they had been worn to the bone, so to speak, by the scouring action of sand, wind and sun, and were shorn of leaves, bark and cones, they still retained the shape of a tree. But they were so stark, so agonized, so done to death that these areas were known locally as *los Corrales de las Cruces*, the Hollows of the Crosses, for to the devout people of the region each of the trees resembled nothing so much as the Cross of the Crucifixion. Farther on, however, the stone pine woods were still intact; the forward

A Mediterranean mongoose trots across the sandy scrub of the Coto Doñana reserve in southern Spain. In summer, the mongoose moves farther inland to the drying marshlands of Las Marismas, where it supplements its usual diet— rats, snakes, lizards and insects—with ducklings and other young water birds.

edge of the living sands had only just reached them, licking like a tongue among the trees and leaning against the trunks. These intact *corrales* were the oases of the dune desert. They were shady and cool, and they contained signs of animal life.

At first they were no more than signs—droppings, feathers and a complex pattern of tracks in the sand which indicated, like traces on a radar screen, where the outriders of the Coto's vast host of wild creatures skirmished in their battle for survival. To decode the cryptic messages left in the sand was difficult. Of the traces I could identify, only four were characteristic of the zone—those of a natterjack toad, a snake (probably Lataste's viper), a hare and a beetle. Two others probably belonged to interlopers from the scrubland farther inland: a deer (almost certainly a red deer), a cat (probably a lynx) and a dog-like animal (most likely a fox). Others again were indecipherable: confused scufflings indicating young animals' play or a fight to the death.

Many reptiles have colonized the *corrales*, where a struggle for living space continues without quarter. Regular inhabitants are two species of lizard (the spiny-toed lizard and the Algerian sand lizard), two species of snake (the Montpellier snake and Lataste's viper) and one species of tortoise (the spur-thighed tortoise *Testudo graeca*). I glimpsed lizards of both species from time to time, scuttling to cover among the Halimium bushes at the landward end of the dunes—brown streaks like snakes on wheels, panic incarnate. Both the Montpellier snake and Lataste's viper hunt in the dunes, and both are poisonous—but to man only the latter is dangerous. The Montpellier snake reaches six feet in length, and on rare occasions even seven feet. In the *corrales* it devours dormice, pine voles and brown rats and it has a voracious appetite—two full-grown rabbits were once found in the stomach of a freshly killed specimen. Its venom can kill a lizard in three to four minutes, but because its poison fangs are set far back in its upper jaw, it has to draw its victim into its mouth before it can inject a fatal dose, so it is unlikely ever to harm a human being. The Lataste's viper, on the other hand, is quite capable of giving a man a nasty bite.

I never saw the Lataste's viper but I did see a small Montpellier snake in the Halimium scrub, a most exquisite creature of olive green and brown, with an ice-cold manner and eyes that gleamed darkly, like polished obsidian. All the other snakes of the Coto—the hooded snake, the Spanish grass snake, the viperine snake, the ladder snake and the little smooth snake—are harmless. The commonest of them is the viperine snake, a relative of the grass snake, and I was to see several

The Spanish imperial eagle, one of
rarest birds in Europe, has its chief
nesting ground in the Coto Doñana.
Above, in a bulky stick nest at the
top of a holm oak tree, an adult
of the species offers meat—probably
the remains of a small mammal—to its
downy young. At this stage, the eaglet
is helpless and sleeps most of the day.
But soon it will move around in the
nest, exercising its limbs. At about two
months (right), it is almost fully grown,
and will soon make its first flight.

individuals of this species along the margins of Las Marismas.

The large population of reptiles, rodents and insects in the *corrales* gives rise to the correspondingly large population of predatory birds. On the ground, under the stone pines of the *corrales*, I found everywhere the regurgitated pellets of these predatory birds, packed with the hard, chitinous remains of small beetles and the tiny undigested teeth and jaws of small reptiles and mammals. As much as a third of all the birds breeding in the stone-pine woods are predatory—including carrion crows, ravens, hobbies, black kites, buzzards, booted eagles, kestrels, short-toed eagles and a few pairs of rare and marvellous Spanish imperial eagles. In winter the residents are joined by visitors like the golden eagle, Bonelli's eagle, ospreys, marsh harriers and peregrines. In all, out of 38 diurnal species of predatory birds in Europe, two dozen are found regularly in the wilderness of the Guadalquivir Delta and most have been recorded at one time or another. Sometimes, on hot afternoons, the black vulture visits the dunes to sleep, and I believe one of the largest and most unnerving footprints I saw in the sand was made by such a bird; the wind had enlarged the original print to the size of an ostrich's claw mark.

Every zone of the Coto Donaña provided new things to discover. Beyond the last of the *corrales* the dunes began to peter out. Ahead of me now the landscape opened up into a broad vista of Halimium scrub followed by dry savannah dotted with scattered umbrella pines and cork oaks, where buzzards and kites soared on the warm thermals. After the scorching confines of the dunes, the wide, open spaces of the plains were a welcome relief. The water of a lake glittered in the middle distance. It was the Laguna de Santa Olalla, the largest of the seven lakes (probably remnants of an ancient arm of the Guadalquivir that had been overrun by the sand) marking the divide between the stone pines and the heathland.

There were still several miles of heath to cross before I reached the destination of my day's journey, the Palacio de Doñana. The afternoon was beginning to fade towards dusk as I set out, and I hurried my steps, disturbing kites and buzzards and azure-winged magpies from the occasional cork-oak trees, and sending little red-breasted Dartford warblers, the commonest bird of these heaths, flitting to cover.

It was then that I saw a huge bird-shape ascend in the eastern sky and begin to soar in wide circles. I knew that a few Spanish imperial eagles were nesting in the stone pines in the south-east corner of the Coto, but I had not dared hope that I might set eyes on one of these rare and magnificent birds. Its sudden appearance was therefore all the more a delight to me. I watched it with admiration as it circled slowly upwards on its immense, outstretched, raptor wings, and flew with an unhurried gravity that seemed to indicate total authority. When a couple of lesser birds of prey took off and began to soar too, the eagle completed one big circle before they completed a small one. The lesser birds huffed and puffed in the lower air, but I am sure that not a single pair of eyes on the ground, human or animal, was looking at them; all eyes were on the eagle, whose majestic gyrations were the most superb example of bird flight that I had ever seen.

The Spanish imperial eagle is a rare sub-species. It is confined to southern Iberia and a few parts of Morocco, and is distinguished from the imperial eagle of eastern Europe by the striking, snow-white markings on the leading edge of its wings. These markings are clearly visible even from a distance and enabled me positively to identify the bird in flight. It is essentially a bird of the plains and for this reason it is more vulnerable than the eagles of the inaccessible mountains—doubly so because its nests are such huge and obvious contraptions in the low stone pines and can easily be raided by collectors of birds' eggs.

It was dusk when I finally reached the Palacio de Doñana, a simple, dignified white building set round a cobbled courtyard and a well, and fronted by a massive, old oak door. Goya is said to have gone there in 1797 and painted the naked Maja, the Duchess of Alba; and King Alfonso XIII of Spain used to stay there in the 1920s, in the days when it was still an aristocratic hunting lodge. Today the Palacio is a base for scientists who wish to study the surrounding wilderness. It is situated on the boundary between heath and marsh, and it therefore marked the limits of my travels in the drylands of southern Spain. The next day I would set out from there into the wetlands of Las Marismas.

The Ceaseless Cycle of Erosion

Whether along Europe's sea-lashed shores or far inland, water is continuously reshaping the continent. Even the toughest rocks must eventually succumb to the water's incessant attack, wearing away grain by grain to eventual nothingness. Now, in the instant of geological time that this century represents, coastlines and mountains stand everywhere in states of semi-destruction: intricate or monumental, smoothly rounded, jagged or irregular.

The infinite variety of forms that water can conjure out of geological materials is governed partly by the diverse behaviour of the water itself —waves, streams, rainstorms—and partly by the varying qualities of the rock it acts upon.

The most minute variations in the structure of a rock can be exploited by water over the passage of many millennia. A set of hair-line fractures, a vanishingly small difference in the solubility of the cement binding sand grains together, a minimal alteration in grain size between one layer of sandstone and the next are all that is required to yield quite different results.

Along the coasts, the waves are constantly at work on rocks both hard and soft. Many of Europe's cliffs are carved from sedimentary rocks laid down beneath the sea millions of years ago. As today's waves wash over them, sand grains that were carried down to the sea by some ancient river are exhumed briefly, then seized by offshore currents and transported away, to be re-deposited perhaps in still, deep waters where they may be bound up in newly forming rock.

Inland, rainfall and streams eat away at the mountains and plateaux, carrying away the particles to form fertile valleys and flat, marshy river deltas. The dramatic effects of streams, as they collect abrasive debris during their descent, were noted more than four centuries ago by the German scientist Georgius Agricola: "Small brooks, which at first only superficially wash the surface of the soil, cut deeper into the hard rock and in time can move great boulders. . . . The more the waters work their way into the depths, the higher the mountains rise on both sides."

Much of Europe's rainfall soaks down through the soil and in limestone areas its solvent action carves out many underground caves and galleries through which subterranean streams may flow. It is here, below the surface, that water creates some of its most exotic effects.

The wave-cut stack called North Haulton Castle, in the Orkneys, rises from the foam just off the hard sandstone coast of which it once formed a part. It was severed from its parent headland by the collapse of caves hollowed out behind it by the sea. Grit-laden waves will continue to erode the angular pinnacle until it, too, topples into the sea.

Rain above and waves below have eaten back the cliffs of the Mediterranean island of Gozo, near Malta (above), throwing into relief a few hard layers that seam the soft sandstone. Tumbled on the shore lie boulders broken from these layers as waves undercut the cliffs.

A closer view of Gozo's shore (right) shows how waves have licked the soft young sandstone of the Mediterranean into characteristic curved forms, further shaped by wind-borne sand. Hardened seams of the iron oxide that gives the rock its yellow colour thread this 30-foot-long natural sculpture.

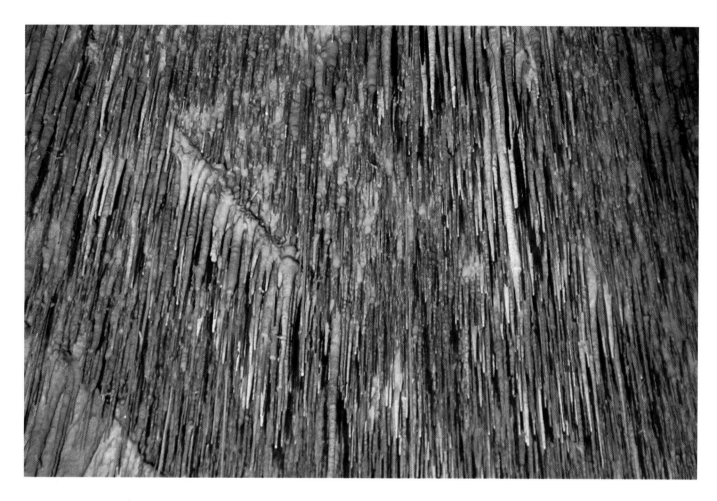

A spray of stalactites (above) hangs
stiffly from the roof of a limestone
cave in the mountains of Majorca.
The fine straws slowly grew as drips of
water came through the porous roof of
the cave, evaporated and deposited
their rich content of calcium carbonate.

A stream has sliced a deep and
shadowy gorge down through the
limestone strata of Majorca's
mountains (left). In the far wall gapes
the mouth of an underground stream-
bed, one of many that find their way
through these rock formations.

Cave-like holes (left) honeycomb a rock face at Meteora in the Thessalian hills of central Greece. These strange galleries, probably formed as rivulets sought out minute differences in the hardness of the sandstone surface, creating small hollows which were then enlarged by wind-driven swirls of sand.

Both wind and water have left their marks on Meteora's monumental humps and cones of grey sandstone (above), which rise to as much as 300 feet. The wind has honed and rounded the rocks, and their horizontal pattern of stratification is criss-crossed by rain-cut gullies and runnels.

Vertically falling rain has created these magnificent earth pillars in the South Tyrol from clay deposited by a melting glacier. Unlike graded river sediment, glacial debris is heaped together in all sizes, and here large stones, uncovered by the rain, act as umbrellas to protect the material beneath. The spires, often known as wigwams, reach heights of 60 feet, but once the umbrella boulders fall, the clay structures are rapidly eroded until another boulder is uncovered and a new, lower spire is produced.

6/ The Wild Marshes

The utter loneliness and desolation of the middle marismas are a sensation to be remembered. Hour after hour one pushes forward across the flooded plains, only to bring within view more and yet more vistas of watery waste and endless horizons of tawny water. ABEL CHAPMAN AND WALTER BUCK/ *WILD SPAIN*

Early in the morning after my arrival at the Palacio de Doñana, I gained my first overall view of Las Marismas, the marshes of the Guadalquivir Delta. A thicket of tall eucalyptus trees sheltered the Palacio at the front, and carefully concealed among the trees was an observation tower 150 feet high, the tallest structure for miles around. I climbed the tower and looked out across the marshes. They seemed to reach to the edge of the world—and the world was flat. From my vantage point I could see as far as the horizon 15 miles or more away, and no outstanding feature, natural or man-made, rose above the skyline or broke up the level monotony of the landscape. For 43 miles the marshes stretched to the north, for 25 miles from east to west—a seasonal, shallow lake separated from the Atlantic by the coastal dunes and scrubland. In winter, after the rains, floodwaters cover the whole of Las Marismas and reach as far as the shoreline of permanently dry land on which the Palacio stands; but it was late June now, and under the hot Andalucian sun the waters had receded.

Between me and the present water's edge lay an expanse of dried-out marsh-bed: churned-up mud that had set like concrete, interspersed with clumps of tall grasses. In the middle distance a broad belt of reeds marked a region of permanent flooding where one of the Guadalquivir's tributaries flowed through the marsh. Far away, one or two barely perceptible patches of dun-coloured, slightly raised ground indicated the position of *vetas*—islands of permanently dry land that provide refuges for foraging animals and nesting birds, and resting places for the *guardas* of the Coto, men who have been brought up in the region and know it as well as anyone.

Las Marismas are one of the few European marshes to have escaped intensive development by man. Many of them—like the Po Delta and the immense Pripet marshes of western Russia—have been drained. Those that survive are mainly in the river deltas of southern Europe—notably part of the Camargue, in the Rhône Delta; the delta of the Danube, in Romania (*see Nature Walk, pages 144-155*); the delta of the Volga, in the U.S.S.R.; and, of course, Las Marismas. In addition, there are several important inland marshes, including the Neusiedlersee in Austria, Lake Kisbalaton in Hungary, the Masurian lakes and the wild expanse of the Biebrzanskie marshes in Poland.

Of all these remaining wetlands, perhaps the most famous is the Camargue. It is famous for its cowboys and gypsies, its semi-wild black bulls and white horses, its one-and-half-inch-long Etruscan shrew (the smallest mammal in Europe, possibly in the world), and its vast concourse of birds—above all its flamingoes, who use the Camargue as their only regular breeding ground in Europe.

I have been to the Camargue, and to the Danube Delta, whose reedbeds are the most extensive in the world; but for me Las Marismas are the most exhilarating—and the most poignant—of Europe's wetlands. These marshes of southern Spain are a crucial intercontinental air junction where bird travellers, particularly waterfowl, arrive from as far away as the tropics and the poles. Two hundred species of birds regularly use the region to rest or feed or breed during their complex seasonal migrations between Africa, Asia and northern Europe. From the Congo comes the purple heron, from Gambia the egret, from Angola the stork, from Ethiopia the bee-eater, from Morocco the hoopoe. To Scotland goes the woodcock, to Denmark the greylag goose, to England the robin, to northern Siberia the widgeon. Without Las Marismas the fate of many bird species would be most uncertain.

I had travelled across the sand and scrub of the Coto Doñana on foot. But clearly feet would not be of much use when I set off into the wet and mud of Las Marismas. In winter or spring it is possible to voyage through the marshes in punts drawn by oxen, but in the drier times of the year a horse is the only satisfactory means of transport. So, with some anxiety—for I had ridden a horse only once before—I had obtained horses and a *guarda* as a guide.

The brackish marshes of Las Marismas, inland from the Gulf of Cadiz, cover more than two-thirds of the Guadalquivir River delta. The marshes are almost wholly flooded during autumn and winter (this photograph was taken in January) and provide a vital stopping point for waterbirds— such as ducks, geese and herons— migrating from northern Europe.

The horses came at nine. The *guarda* who brought them was a friendly, burly Andalucian with a voice like a loud-hailer and a face darkened to the colour of walnut by the sun and the wind. His name was Francisco Espina, but he was known to everyone as Curro, which means both "pretty" and "loud". He wore a caballero's grey riding suit, and his head was enveloped in a chequered white cloth to keep out the flies and the sun. On top of the cloth sat a grey, round sombrero. Curro was born to the saddle and these open skies, and he knew the names of all the plants and birds and animals, and their habits.

Curro handed me the reins of a placid-looking nag and I swung my right foot up into the broad metal stirrup. The important thing was not to fall off on the other side.

"*Segunda vez,*" I explained, apologizing in advance for my ineptitude on horseback. "This is only my second time on a horse, you know."

Curro nodded. "*Monte! monte!*" he roared. "Get on!"

I remembered my first experience on a horse with some distaste. It was in a remote part of the Mato Grosso in Brazil. The horse was a highly pregnant mare and I felt quite secure in her ill-fitting saddle. But at the first opportunity she had veered off the track and into the forest to graze, leaving me suspended from the first low branch that barred my way. I had been horse-borne in the Mato Grosso for ten minutes; here in Las Marismas I would have to sit in the saddle for ten hours to conduct a satisfactory tour. I swung my left foot over and sat in the saddle. I nudged the nag's ribs with my heels and we lurched into motion.

My aim was to explore as much of Las Marismas, the various habitats and bird colonies, as the hours of daylight would allow. Our route, therefore, was to be a circuitous one, taking in the localities Curro believed to be of greatest interest to me and having as its final objective the lake called Lucio de Mari-López, where a flamingo flock was known to be feeding. We would start out north-west along the shoreline of Las Marismas, then head north across the now dried-up marsh-bed to the still flooded region in the centre beyond the Guadiamar River; after that we would swing east and then south to the flamingo lake, before returning to the Palacio Doñana in the south-west. Such a round tour would take us through three wilderness zones of the National Park of the Coto Doñana: first, part of Las Marismas, then the Marismas de Hinojos, and finally the Reserva de Guadiamar, an inland adjunct of the National Park.

I would not see Las Marismas at their most prolific, I was told before I set out. The summer was too advanced, and in any case the rains had failed the previous autumn so that the water level was exceptionally low and many birds were not breeding. I took these admonitions to heart; and yet, by the time I returned from my horse patrol later that day, I brought back with me a picture of a swooping, shrieking, skulking bird metropolis where often there was barely room for the horses to put their hoofs. It was a blurred and confused picture, as though the wind and the sun and the vast sky had somehow dizzied my brain.

North-west of the Palacio, on the edge of Las Marismas, stand a group of ancient cork oak trees with bark like whale blubber. Among tall thickets of gorse and fern, they spread out their bare, sturdy limbs for the birds. Enormous colonies of spoonbills and herons and egrets nest in these trees, screaming and squabbling and scattering like a spray of white feathers from a burst pillow. With one exception, every European type of heron and heron-like bird breeds in the Coto, and Curro never ceased to shout their Spanish names, "*Garza real!*" he yelled. "*Garza imperial! Garcilla cangrejera! Garceta común!*" Heron and purple heron, squacco heron and little egret—they have nested in the Coto since prehistory. But the spoonbills, with beaks like elongated castanets and long, white crests like the plumes of an imperial governor's hat, only began nesting here in the 1960s.

At the cork oak trees we left the littoral of dry land and headed our horses north across a broad stretch of dried-out Salicornia heath, the

savannah-like country that in summer covers most of Las Marismas. This stretch, Curro said with a wave of the hand, was called Bonanza. It never ceased to amaze me that a landscape apparently so featureless should bear so many place names. Every slight dip, every slight rise, every clump of reeds or patch of mud seemed to have a name.

Bonanza, explained Curro, was where he had once encountered that rare and elusive carnivore, the lynx. It was trying to subdue a great greylag goose. Hoping to get it photographed, Curro had galloped back to the Palacio and shouted for a distinguished naturalist, photographer and *aficionado* of the Coto who was staying there at the time, Dr. Juan Fernández. Together they galloped towards Bonanza and arrived in time to find the lynx still wrestling with the goose. "And that," said Curro, "was how the photograph was taken." (It appears on the opposite page.) The little clump of trees shimmering on the horizon far out in Las Marismas, Curro added, was an island called Veta de la Arena, the limit of his territory. There I would find a new *guarda*.

We headed towards the island, two lonely figures in the immense solitude of Las Marismas, and the sun rose higher in the empty sky and the birds soared and swooped. We flushed wild boars and herds of fallow deer from clumps of grass and sedge. The dried-out marsh-bed gave way to damper ground as we neared the small permanent stream called Madre de las Marismas. The horses squelched through mud and then splashed into a broad area of shallow marsh, set here and there with clumps of tall reeds and bulrushes. We crossed the stream and entered the Marismas de Hinojos. Here the water was a foot deep on average, and reached three to four feet in the deepest parts.

It was clear within a very short while that this was a favourite spot for waterbirds, which had probably come here for the seeds and grasses and aquatic organisms that teemed in the muddy water. The air was thick with whiskered terns—exquisite, swallow-like marsh birds with black caps and dark-red bills and feet, who, in a demonstration of tetchy irritability, dived at us and shrilly shrieked at us, trying to drive us off. The water was alive with ducks, and with their noisy complaints and clattering wingbeats. The horses sploshing by put them into a great commotion and they paddled hectically for the cover of the reeds or rose as a flock into the sky, trailing beads of glittering waterdrops as they wheeled above us. Mostly they were mallards and gadwalls, but I noticed a few red-crested pochard, the drakes outstanding with their bright chestnut heads. In winter, at the time of maximum flooding of Las Marismas, up to a third of a million ducks

As described in the text, a greylag goose in Las Marismas has fallen victim to an invader from the coastal dunes and scrub: a rare Spanish lynx.

seek refuge here from the freezing latitudes of Scandinavia and Siberia: teals, pintails, shovellers, scoters, as well as the mallards and gadwalls.

A good idea of the prodigality of the winter bird population is given by the "bags" recorded by hunters in the days before the Coto Doñana was a nature reserve. In a single day in December, 1905, for example, the English hunter-naturalist Walter Buck, one of the first men seriously to study Las Marismas, killed 273 waterfowl with a 12-bore shotgun. Even more astonishing, in 1943 the head gamekeeper at the Palacio was handed four cartridges and asked to get something for dinner. Half an hour later he returned with three unused cartridges and 27 teal that had fallen to a single shot aimed into the crowded sky.

We reached drier ground on the other side of the Marismas de Hinojos, where the land sloped gently up towards the Veta de la Arena. The island was inhabited. Behind a reed enclosure similar to a Masai zariba lay two or three reed-and-grass huts of the sort you see in the interior of Africa. In front of the huts stood a reception committee of half a dozen *guardas*. One was better dressed than the others and held himself with an almost military bearing. He stepped forward and took my reins. His name was Pepe Clarida, the *guarda* of the Lucio de Mari-López, the flamingo lake. I could not have met a better man.

I was invited into a hut and offered coffee or wine. "You can't have both!" roared Curro, and I took coffee. Curro delivered me into the capable hands of Pepe, and after a few minutes of desultory conversation, I shook hands with my hospitable hosts and set off with Pepe.

The island descended imperceptibly towards the floodland of the Guadiamar River. We put up a covey of pin-tailed sand grouse and were dive-bombed by another colony of outraged whiskered terns, who screeched and stabbed at us in an immense communal tantrum. The sky was a great rotunda within whose far horizons we were trapped like spiders in an inverted bell-jar. We rode on and on into the interior of Las Marismas, and the landmarks of the western shore vanished one by one below the skyline. We did not speak much, for speech was superfluous, and a great silence descended on us, broken only by the snorting of the horses and the jingle of their bits as they tossed their heads.

As we approached the Guadiamar River, the horses' hoofs brought up clouds of rusty-looking mud and a stench of river bottom and rotten vegetation. In the channel of the river, which was hard to detect except by the depth of our immersion, the water reached up to the horses' haunches and covered my legs up to the knees. Las Marismas are full of

Half hidden in the glasswort scrub of Las Marismas, a resting purple gallinule is readily identified by its bright red bill. The purple gallinule is an inquisitive bird and often comes out of hiding to peer at whatever is passing—one reason perhaps why the species is now rare in Europe.

leeches; 40 or 50 can fasten on to a man in half an hour and draw blood. But my immersion was too brief to allow these repulsive creatures to get a hold on me and we were quickly into the Reserva de Guadiamar.

There was a great abundance of coots here, and mallards, garganey and red-crested pochards, some with little chicks bobbing about among the reeds. Pepe constantly jumped from his saddle to run through the swamps in pursuit of ducks to ring, for the ringing of birds to determine their seasonal movements is an important part of the research work in the Coto reserves. We passed large colonies of black-winged stilts, the predominant bird of this part of Las Marismas, their nests built on platforms low down in the reeds near the surface of the water. We passed avocets, graceful black-and-white birds with long legs, a fastidious gait and long, upturned bills; and the nests of redshanks with three or four pear-shaped, spotted, buff-coloured eggs in them; and baby bitterns that froze among the reeds as we drew near, their necks and beaks pointing into the sky so as to merge with the reeds as they stood in their crude, untidy nests on the water.

I began to feel that I was intruding, that I was somehow trespassing among these bird ghettoes, these waterfowl tenements with their bed-sits, nurseries and paddling pools; nests, eggs and chicks were often so dense underfoot and so skilfully concealed that I became concerned that my horse should not crush them. In the marshes and on the small *vetas* of raised land there were grebes, turnstones, knots, curlews, sandpipers, ruffs, dunlins, black-tailed godwits, plovers of various kinds, and always overhead the angry terns—whiskered, little and black. Just about the only bird of Las Marismas I did not see was the oddest: the rare purple gallinule, like an ungainly, overgrown coot, with a big red beak and big red feet, and a maniacal hooting shriek.

After leaving the Reserva de Guadiamar, we came at last to the Lucio de Mari-López, the flamingo lake. There were, so Pepe said, one to two thousand flamingoes on the lake—greater flamingoes, *Phoenicopterus ruber*—and from where I stood 300 yards away they seemed to occupy the entire surface of the water. A strange, unending, grumbling sound came from them, like the muttering of a football crowd whose home team is losing. Through binoculars the whole concourse of birds looked like a stampede of learned dons—a bustling, surging, ill organized to-ing and fro-ing of long, stiff, skinny legs. This way and that the birds plodded, heads bent low as their beaks sifted the shallow water for food. When we drew nearer, a collective alarm shivered through the flock and they began to riffle their wings in preparation for take-off. As they did so, the colour of the flock changed from white to brilliant pink, and a roseate electronic oscillation seemed to emanate from them, a sort of vibrating haze; but when we moved off they stopped fluttering, and once they had sheathed their wings the flock turned white again.

The flamingoes are drawn to Las Marismas by the high salinity of its water, which suits their feeding requirements, and since 1977 they have been observed breeding here. Perhaps they are the dwindling remnant of a population that has been breeding elsewhere, or perhaps they come here from the Camargue for a change of feeding ground or to rest when they are on their way to Africa. But no one knows for certain. The movements of flamingoes between different countries have never been properly observed and a great deal of mystery still surrounds these birds.

We set off from the lake of Mari López and reached dry land again, turning towards the Palacio, invisible still below the western horizon. The sun was past its zenith now, the light of late afternoon less harsh.

"Don't you ever get lonely living out here?" I asked Pepe.

He turned in his saddle and fixed his steady gaze on me. "Yes," he said. "But when I do, I come out to watch the flamingoes and then I'm not lonely any more."

And his hand described a wide circle to enclose the territory that was his home—the prairie of green-yellow waving grass, the birds wheeling in the great space, the oasis mirages of stone pines on the shimmering edge of the continent.

"*Bonito*, eh?" he said again, with a simple but passionate pride.

"*Bonito*."

We plodded on, each sunk in his own thoughts. Pepe at length broke into a grave *cante jondo*—a deep song of the south, sung in an ancient mode, half Arabic, half Hebraic, and melancholic and intense. The words were strangely familiar: "*Si oyes doblar la campana*," he sang, "*no pregunte quien ha muerto. . . .*" ("If you hear the bell toll, do not ask who is dead. . . .")

He sang quietly to himself, deep in his throat, so that the song drifted across to me sporadically, rising and falling in the wind. And I suddenly felt very sad. I was grateful for the privilege of seeing this beautiful place, and the wild places in other parts of Europe still as they were when they were made. But would my children see them, would my children's children? Would they ever see this place as I had seen it today, the birds flying free, the animals running wild?

Close to the Palacio, at the edge of a reed-rimmed pond full of coots, are the laboratories of the Coto Doñana. The director of the reserve is

Dr. Castroviejo, a very likeable and energetic young scientist, with a profound but unsentimental love of living things and a deep concern for the future of the delta's wildlife. I asked him what the prospects for the Coto Doñana and Las Marismas were, in view of the pressures now being put on all the wild places of Europe.

"You know, I am not a pessimist," he replied. "I am a realist. I know where a place like the Coto stands in the world's list of priorities, in Spain's list of priorities. The Coto now is not what it was even 15 years ago. Some bird species have disappeared since then, some are on the point of disappearing. If you ask me what it will be like 15 years from now—well, sometimes I am greatly afraid."

For centuries, Dr. Castroviejo explained, the Guadalquivir Delta had been virtually unknown to the rest of Europe. No systematic attention was given to its wildlife until the last quarter of the 19th Century, when the English hunter-naturalists Abel Chapman and Walter Buck explored the region regularly every season for 20 years or more and published their accounts in two books, *Wild Spain* (1893) and *Unexplored Spain* (1910). Although the books were widely read, the discomforts of travel deterred any spate of visitors, and the delta remained a forgotten corner of Europe until the 1950s, when it became world famous as a result of three Anglo-Spanish scientific expeditions led by the British ornithologist Guy Mountfort.

During the course of these expeditions it was discovered that the existence of the delta as a wildlife sanctuary was threatened. A large part of the Coto, which was then in private hands, was to be sold as development land and much of Las Marismas was to be drained. The expeditions contained men of international stature—men like the eminent biologist, Sir Julian Huxley; and Churchill's wartime Chief of Staff, Field Marshal Lord Alanbrooke, an ardent ornithologist. These and other like-minded men in many countries decided that they could not stand idly by and watch a place like the Coto Doñana be destroyed. They decided they must try to buy the Coto before the developers did. The World Wildlife Fund was founded in 1961, and with the proceeds of a world-wide public appeal and a grant from the Spanish government, its organizers were eventually able to complete the purchase of the Coto Doñana. In 1964 the new nature reserve was officially opened under its first Director, Dr. José Antonio Valverde, an outstanding Spanish member of the 1950 expeditions.

At that time it seemed that much of the Coto and Las Marismas had been saved for posterity; but now the future no longer seems so certain.

I asked Dr. Castroviejo about the latest problems. As I spoke, an assistant came in bringing the shattered remains of a spur-thighed tortoise that had just been run over by a car. Dr. Castroviejo took the creature in his hand. *"Pobre animal!"* he exclaimed. "It was not the driver's fault, he was driving very carefully. It wasn't the tortoise's fault, he didn't know about cars. It was just that the two were incompatible, and you can see who won. I fear the reserve is like the tortoise. It is beautiful, it does nobody any harm. It has a right to exist. But it will be destroyed. You know, sometimes I feel like Don Quixote—I turn to deal with one danger and another one appears behind my back."

The Coto now faced several threats. There was a proposal to build a coastal motorway linking Huelva and Cadiz which would cut along the dunes of the Coto; and there was every danger that *urbanización* would spread along the coast from the new tourist resort known as Matalascañas, a sprawling town on the north-west margins of the Coto where at the height of the season 50,000 well-oiled North Europeans slowly revolve in the sun. Birds and animals who strayed into the town from the Coto were shot by waiters. Cats and dogs that strayed out of town killed the wildlife in the Coto. Holidaymakers set fire to the dry heathland and stole the eggs from the imperial eagles' nests. At the last count there were only 60 to 80 pairs of Spanish imperial eagles left in Spain, of which the greatest concentration—12 breeding pairs—were in the Coto. Each pair needs nearly ten square miles of land to hunt over in summer, and more in winter. While it is possible to protect them in their breeding area, it is not possible to do so when they stray outside, as they must do. When the development market turns up and building starts again, the whole of the Coto may be cut off from the sea by a string of new beach resorts from Matalascañas to the Guadalquivir, and the eagles and spoonbills and other wild birds migrating to and from Africa will have to run the gauntlet of high-density urban humanity.

There were several dangers to the waters of Las Marismas. If a proposed dam were built across the Guadalquivir, it could drastically change the water level and the salinity of the marshes. The pyrites mines at Aznalcollar, to the north of Las Marismas, were putting waste into the Guadiamar River and in due course this pollution could have adverse effects. Insecticides from the rice fields along the Brazo de la Torre, an arm of the Guadalquivir, had already been carried down into one of the largest permanent lakes, the Lucio de las Ansares, poisoning the waterfowl and causing their eggs to be laid with abnormally thin shells, so that the number of successfully hatched chicks

Two spoonbills and a little egret (bottom right) perch together in the outer branches of a holm oak at the edge of Las Marismas. These species often share the same nesting quarters, and particularly favour the holm oak because it grows close to the muddy waters where aquatic insects, worms, snails and fish abound.

was considerably reduced. Herbicides were also tipped into the rice fields so as to kill off the *castañuela* plant, a kind of bulrush called sea clubrush (*Scirpus maritimus*), the dominant wild plant of Las Marismas. Its roots are like little chestnuts and constitute the main food of geese and ducks there.

In addition, since the 1950s there have been persistent attempts by the Ministry of Agriculture to drain Las Marismas and transform the wilderness into a vast market garden. This particular onslaught underlines the unresolvable dilemma, the conflict of interests that bedevils the future of all the wild places. It is a story as old as the human race: the battle between the needs of man and the needs of nature. The establishment in the late 1960s of the National Park of the Coto Doñana saved a major part of the marshes, and plans to drain other sectors have now fortunately been shelved. But man-made changes are not the only threat, since the long-term forecast seems to indicate a natural reduction in the extent of flooding and salinity of Las Marismas, which will vitally affect the birds.

"I don't know what will happen to the Coto," Dr. Castroviejo told me. "Birds like the glossy ibis, the crested coot, the crane and the white-headed duck have gone already. The ferruginous duck has virtually gone. And the shelduck, the marbled teal and the slender-billed gull are going. The number of pairs of imperial eagles decreased by 30 to 50 per cent between 1950 and 1970—they were laying a lot of infertile eggs."

I walked with Dr. Castroviejo back up the sandy track to the Palacio. The spoonbills and herons of the cork tree colonies just to the north were coming back to roost from their foraging expeditions.

"People say, what does it matter—a few ducks having a hard time? What about all the people in the world who are having a hard time?" Dr. Castroviejo stopped and turned to me. "And I say to them, it does matter. It matters if a duck dies of poison and if a man dies of hunger. Because all life is related, all things are connected. The fact that we are human beings does not mean that we are separate from the other living things of this planet. If we are prepared to let the creatures of the Coto die, then we are ultimately prepared to let people die, too."

We reached the Palacio. For four centuries it had looked out over an unchanged vista, across a primeval world as free and untramelled as on the day of its creation.

"This is one of the last wildernesses in southern Europe," Dr. Castroviejo continued, "but the impact of civilization has been brutal. And there is little we can do about it. If we stop the poisoned rivers flowing into Las Marismas, the water level will drop and the wildlife will decline. If the rivers continue to flow, the wildlife will be poisoned. Either way it will one day spell the end of this wonderful place."

After supper on my last night in the Coto I walked out of the Palacio into the country around. It was a magnificent night, warm and clear, the sky glittering with stars. The wind had dropped, and the air was still and full of faint voices: birds calling, frogs croaking, animals shuffling in the shadows—sounds as elusive and fragmentary as the tracks in the dunes. I had known such nights as this in the African bush, but rarely, if ever, in Europe. A feeling of profound peace settled over me, as though the world inside my skin had achieved complete equilibrium with the world outside it, an absolute harmony.

I walked on down a sandy trail. Eight fallow deer stirred in a clearing wanly lit by a half-moon. Far away a night-jar churred. And then I was stopped dead in my tracks. The back of my neck tingled and I did not move. A loud and terrible cry drowned all other sounds; it reached a crescendo, was held, then died slowly away, receding across the dark spaces to the edge of the world. The cry was repeated, longer and louder this time, and then again.

Three wolves had been saved from slaughter in the sierras and brought to the Coto for safe keeping. They lived in a large pen near the Palacio, and my nocturnal prowl had disturbed them. I had never heard wolves howling before and I would probably never hear them howling again. The wolf was the arch-enemy of my species, European man's most deadly animal competitor, the primeval wilderness incarnate. And now it was almost done for. These three wolves were remnants of a dying race. I stood and listened to that terrible cry. It seemed to fill the night with a defiant anguish, with a vast and savage sorrow.

NATURE WALK / Through the Danube Delta

TEXT BY JOHN A. BURTON

PHOTOGRAPHS BY DOUGLAS BOTTING

In the chill grey mists of a late September dawn, I made my way with Douglas Botting—on this trip in his capacity of photographer—to the quay in the tiny Romanian village of Sfintu Gheorghe. The mission we had set ourselves was a day's tour of the largest wetland wilderness left in the continent of Europe: the Danube Delta.

This 2,000-square-mile expanse of reed-beds, waterways, islands and shallow open water is formed—and continually added to—by the millions of tons of silt that the Danube carries annually into the Black Sea. It is a huge wildlife haven whose predominantly fresh waters teem with nearly 100 varieties of fish. Over 160 breeding species of birds—for me the most compelling reason for our visit—find it a perfect refuge, and its low islands and dry expanses support thickets of willow, poplar, alder and oak that are the haunt of many kinds of animals, some—like wild boar and tree-climbing reed-wolves—of great interest to naturalists.

Our trip was to be by boat, the only way of travelling in much of the delta. Sfintu Gheorghe lies on the southernmost of the three main channels by which the Danube flows through the wetlands, not far from where the delta's outermost edge spreads into the Black Sea. Our plan was to make our way downstream through the reed-beds straight to the sea, and begin by landing on Sahalin, a long, narrow sandbar of an island lying just offshore, separated from the delta's ill-defined edge by a shallow lagoon of open water. After taking a look at the island's coastal sand dunes, we would return inland by stages, visiting first the lagoons and reed-beds of the delta's more recently formed outlying parts, and then the low islands and flat expanses of the drier inland regions. Finally we planned to climb a ruined lighthouse in this drier part, from which we would gain a better view of the wilderness than was possible from anywhere among the reeds.

Down the Main Channel

At the quayside we met Cladiade Panniot, warden of a vast stretch of the delta, and our guide for the day. Low clouds hung overhead, but Cladiade assured us they would soon clear, and we set off down the main channel. Cladiade rowed with even, practised strokes, and we were soon enclosed in a side channel where the only sound was the splash of oars and the rustling of the reeds that spread in every direction.

The sun did appear, and the chill was going from the air. We were deep in the heart of the reed-beds, but so far we had seen little evidence of wildlife. In fact, we were just beginning to doubt if we had picked a good spot to see any birds when there came a twittering, barely audi-

A HOBBY ON ITS PERCH

ble at first over the rustling of the reeds. Then, wave after wave of swallows swept over the boat on their way to winter in Africa.

Suddenly, Cladiade stopped rowing and pointed. "*Falco!*" The bird he had seen was a hobby—one of the smallest birds of prey, with an aerobatic skill that enables it to feed on a variety of smaller birds. Perched in a dead willow, it looked resplendent with blackish hood, rust-red leggings and yellow socks. Suddenly it took off and idly chased a couple of swallows. As the day grew warmer more hobbies appeared, as well as some red-footed falcons, all going south, like the swallows.

A REED-BORDERED CHANNEL

WATER LILIES ALONG THE REED-BEDS

As we followed the leisurely flight of the hobbies our attention was caught by a jewel-like flash of turquoise among the reeds. It was a kingfisher. One of the hobbies gave chase. Hunter and prey twisted and turned for a few seconds before the kingfisher escaped, with a flurry of blue and emerald, into the safety of the reeds. We were now rounding a bend in the channel, and Cladiade signalled for us to keep very quiet. We were leaving the channel, and ahead of us, looking like a large lake, lay the apparently deserted stretch of water that separates the island of Sahalin from the delta. Rushes and whispering reeds swayed gently and the edges of water lilies rippled in the breeze.

A split-second after we nosed into the lake, it exploded with birds.

WATER CHESTNUT

SPIKY WATER CHESTNUT SEEDS

Coots pattered across the water's surface, leaving a trail of ripples; grebes and ducks dived and looped; teals and mallards sprang into the air; screaming terns wheeled and soared. Cladiade let the boat drift while he scanned the water. "*Pelicani*," he announced, pointing to specks on the horizon. Even through my powerful binoculars they looked like swans. Ten minutes later, when we set foot on Sahalin, I could see that they were indeed pelicans. Disturbed by our presence, they flapped lazily past us to settle again further along the island.

The island was sandy, but we were not tempted to take off our sandals, for the ground was littered with barbed seeds of the water chestnut (*Trapa natans*). We had seen these plants floating near by, their leaves decorating the water's surface with regular patterns like those of vast green snowflakes. The water chestnut's seedpod has evolved a useful means of anchoring itself in the mud that has ferocious consequences for anyone who treads unwarily: it is armed with four spikes, so arranged that one or more always catches in the ground—leaving the others to point upwards.

At the spot where we beached the boat and unloaded our gear, the island was barely 100 yards wide. We walked over the low dunes to the outer shore where, under a now cloudless sky, the silt-laden sea was surprisingly rough. Here the massive freshwater outflow of the Danube dilutes the salty water of the

TRACKS OF RACOON-LIKE DOG

Black Sea sufficiently for reeds—mostly of the feathery, plumed kind called phragmites—to grow down to the water's edge.

An Odd Species of Dog

Walking along the tide-line, I noticed some paw-marks in the wet sand. When I asked Cladiade in my pidgin-Romanian if they had been made by a dog, he answered that it was a dog, but of a kind that had come from China through Russia to Romania. I realized that what Cladiade had in mind was a rather odd species: *Nyctereutes procynoides*. It is a member of the dog family, but is like the North American racoon in appearance. Hence its name, which means racoon-like dog. Originally found only in the Far East,

PHRAGMITES REEDS

THE DELTA COAST FROM THE BLACK SEA

these animals were bred in Russia for fur. Some of them escaped from the fur farms and established wild populations. From Russia they spread into the Danube Delta, where they were first seen in 1951.

We crossed back over the sand dunes to the island's landward side and descended into a thick reed-bed, where Cladiade told us to keep well down and walk as silently as possible. He led us on for 100 yards, then stopped and carefully parted the reeds. We were on the shore facing the mainland of the delta. In front of us, roosting on the mud, were our pelicans, about 20 of them. Behind them a flock of whiskered terns slept at the water's edge, undisturbed by the ceaseless scurrying of the many different wading birds probing for food in the shallows. The busy foragers included Kentish plovers, little stints, marsh sand-

WHITE PELICANS

pipers and greenshanks. Scarcely had Douglas cocked his camera when we heard the alarm call of a watchful redshank. The pelicans shuffled uneasily. A moment later, with an ungainly waddle and heavy flapping of wings, one of them took off; then singly or in pairs they all took to the air. Although they look awkward taking off, once they are airborne, they fly with remarkable ease and grace. The slow, powerful beating of their broad wings, followed by a long, relaxed glide, carried them majestically away.

An Abundance of Insects

On this side of the island the breeze had dropped completely and in the warm stillness we noticed the insects. Luckily there were no mosquitoes, but in addition to green bush-crickets and fast-flying red winged-grasshoppers, we now began to see delicately coloured blue, green and red damsel flies resting on plantains and other flowers. Big yellow dragonflies careered past at

WATER-WEED

an incredible speed. Sipping nectar from the plentiful Michaelmas daisies were harmless hover flies—their bold black and yellow markings resembling those of wasps and providing camouflage against inquisitive predators. We wandered on a little way along the muddy shore where the pelicans had been. Occasional strands of water-weed and other vegetation groped through the mud and at every step we saw an amazing number of empty shells, mostly of freshwater snails, which provide the birds with ample sustenance. The shells were mainly of the ram's horn type, but there were also some with spiralled apexes

DAMSEL FLY ON PLANTAIN

RAM'S HORN SNAIL

that had housed great pond snails, and a few that had contained massive freshwater mussels.

As we ambled back along the beach to the boat, the sky was still full of terns streaming past, joined now by gulls. Groups of them circled and descended and we could identify a huge variety of species, among them black-headed, common, herring and slender-billed gulls. Other waders joined them on the mudflats to feed: curlews (including the slender-billed variety, which is virtually unknown in western Europe), marsh sandpipers, black-tailed godwits and a large flock of dunlins, which are closely related to sandpipers.

We sat by the boat to eat the lunch we had brought—fish, the staple diet on the Danube. We looked about us while we ate, and were rewarded by a flight of mute swans passing overhead. Although well-established

MUTE SWAN

in the delta, these swans are wary and are not often seen. The name is rather misleading for, although rarely vocal, they make a whistling sound with their wings which can be heard as they pass overhead.

Finally, washing down our lunch with mineral water—Danube waters

FEEDING DUNLINS

are deemed undrinkable even by the tough locals—we reloaded the boat and pushed out again for the mainland and the next stage of our trip. Bumping occasionally on a sandbar and scooping up mud with our oars, we recrossed the broad expanse of water and again entered the channels of the main delta.

As we threaded our way through the reeds, small birds fluttered about us. One, a beautiful cock redstart, posed half hidden just long enough for Douglas to photograph him. Dunlins, egrets and herons flew up from the margins of the lily-choked creeks. There were grey, purple and squacco herons and great white herons (once highly coveted for their osprey plumes).

We stepped ashore for our visit to the lighthouse. The ground was no more than a few inches above water-level, but a small grove of white willows grew there, providing us with some welcome shade. A hen

A YOUNG RED-BACKED SHRIKE

red-backed shrike looked quizzically at us from a notice board declaring the area a nature reserve, and another shrike flew ahead of us. It was a juvenile bird, probably the female's offspring, and quite fearless: apparently it was unaware as yet that man is a dangerous animal.

We climbed the staircase that wound round the outside of the tower, but only when we clambered

on to the flat wooden roof were we able to appreciate the sheer size of the delta. It was staggering—the more so when we realized from a glance at our maps that what we could see represented only a tiny proportion of the total area. In every direction spread the gently swaying reed-beds with which we had now become so familiar at water level. Occasional willows cast their shadows and, snaking into the distance, were waterways like those along which we had rowed. To the west, the north and the south the reeds spread away unbroken as far as the horizon; to the east lay Sahalin and the Black Sea.

The tower had been built, more than a century ago, as a coastal lighthouse. Now it stood half a mile inland. Nothing could have brought home to us more forcefully the speed with which the delta is spreading. In some places it is increasing at the astonishing rate of more than 400

A COCK REDSTART

WILLOWS AMONG THE REEDS

TWELVE-FOOT HIGH REEDS

feet a year. In another few decades the water between Sahalin and the present edge of the delta will be blanketed with a floating reed-bed, and this in turn will clog and solidify. Then the silt will begin to form another sandbar island off the new shore-line.

Teeming Ground Life

We descended. The young red-backed shrike flew off, alerting a purple heron that eyed us suspiciously from the enveloping reed-beds. Cumbrously it flapped away, its iridescent plumage turning from brownish to true purple in the slanting rays of the still-hot sun. Our horizons closed in again, and we readjusted to the scale of the teeming life within the branches, reeds and ponds at ground level.

The first creature I could see as I looked up into the willow branches was a spotted woodpecker. But a moment later some penduline tits joined it in the treetops to feed. In

A PURPLE HERON

A REED-CHOKED CHANNEL

spring these delightful little birds build elaborate woven nests that hang over the water from the tips of willow branches. This location provides them with security from the delta's many and varied predators.

An Amphibian Ventriloquist

High in the sky migrant birds were still passing, mostly swallows as before, but also large numbers of white wagtails. As we stood watching them, there burst from among the willows the strident and accelerating *kraak-kraak-kraak* of the emerald green tree frog. Only an inch long, and nearly invisible in its habitat, this creature is also an excellent ventriloquist; although I searched carefully I was unable to locate it.

During my search, however, I stumbled across a shallow pond that had almost completely dried up and was alive with other kinds of frogs and toads. All day during our leisurely progress through the overgrown heart of the wilderness, we had seen edible frogs basking on lily pads, only bestirring themselves to plop into the water if the boat crept directly towards them. Now we had a chance to see them at close quarters. Douglas went down on hands and knees to photograph them. The frogs' turned out to be particularly interesting: they seemed to be a hybrid between the edible and the marsh frog, two species that are common in the delta. But unlike both

AN EDIBLE FROG

parent species, which are often large and usually greenish, the hybrids were mainly brown.

Among the frogs there were some baby fire-bellied toads. These rather flat, diminutive creatures are unspectacular when seen from above; but their undersides are marbled a brilliant orange-red and black. When alarmed, they sometimes arch their backs to display these colours—a warning to predators that their skin secretes noxious irritants.

Probing farther into the vegetation, I came upon signs of mammalian life. Hidden in the bulrushes, I found the remains of a fish. It had been killed and partly eaten—perhaps by an otter or a mink, since both are widespread in the delta. A trail of steely scales showed where the fish had been dragged from the water across the mud.

Here was a graphic reminder that, close by, beneath the surface of the water, lay yet another realm of the delta. For most of the day I had had the uneasy feeling that, preoccupied as we were by the immediately visible superabundance of wildlife in this region, we were paying insufficient attention to the hidden world of the fish. I had peered down several times through the clear water and each time I had been amazed at the scene of activity: fish were present in unbelievable numbers. At first I thought I must have found a particularly good spot; but it proved the same wherever I looked, and I was forced to conclude that such profusion was normal. I knew that among the remarkable fish of the delta were the sturgeon of the caviar industry, tiny herrings that can live in fresh water, the spined loach, the

A FIRE-BELLIED TOAD

rapacious carp and the giant catfish, or wels, that has been known to grow to nearly nine feet in length.

But we had no time to seek a closer acquaintance with this rich world beneath the water, and we regretfully decided that, on this trip at least, our first-hand experience of the Danube Delta's fish would have to be confined to eating them.

Douglas had finished photographing the frogs and toads, and caught me up while I was inspecting the remains of the fish. As he recorded it, I also noticed a crested newt. To find one in the autumn requires more than a little luck, for this is the time of their hibernation under logs and stones. I picked it up

A HALF-EATEN FISH

BULRUSHES

and examined it. It was about six inches long and its deep orange belly indicated that it was of a type found only in and around the Danube below Vienna. Those found in other parts of Europe have bright sulphur-yellow undersides.

What other life existed on the borders between earth and water? Bubbles of marsh gas—methane—rising from the shallows drew our attention to another pool, where we found great diving beetles scudding around. They are voracious predators and probably feed mostly on tadpoles spawned by the ever-present frogs.

Suddenly, I spotted several large leeches looping their way through the water, and glancing down I saw that my legs were splotched with dark shapes. The creatures had probably been clinging for some time, yet caused no pain, which is why I had not noticed them before. I pulled them off.

A GREAT DIVING BEETLE

A LEECH

At last, we reluctantly packed our gear back into the boat and set off through the early evening for Sfîntu Gheorghe. As we neared the village quayside from the main channel the cold night air was rising from the water and a few early bats were mingling with the last of the swallows and some night herons.

A Final Wild Reminder

On our way from the quay to supper we had one final, unexpected encounter when we spotted a small creature moving across the main street into an overgrown garden in the light of a street lamp. It was a green toad, whose emerald markings make it for me one of the most beautiful of toads. It was eating the supply of moths attracted by the lamp. Plainly, we could have extended our investigations into the night; but after 12 hours, and with this final reminder of the pervasiveness of wild life in the Danube Delta, we were ready to call it a day.

A CRESTED NEWT

BUBBLING MARSH GAS

A GREEN TOAD

7/To the Western Isles

Yet three score miles—rocks—surge—uninhabited—uncouth
landing places: how to get to it, and upon it—that is
a question! T. S. MUIR/ECCLESIOLOGICAL NOTES ON THE ISLANDS OF SCOTLAND

Ten major seas lap the shores of Europe, each with its own character and coastline. I have seen most of them, from the Arctic Ocean to the Aegean, from the Atlantic to the Black Sea and the Caspian. These seas form Europe's frontier, and no part of that frontier in my experience is wilder or more abundant in natural life than the world enclosed by the waters of the north-east Atlantic—I mean the exhilarating, windswept islands of the Hebrides, or Western Isles, to which in my mind's eye I am compelled to return again and again. The space and light and sense of freedom invoked by these scattered islands is equalled, in my opinion, in few other parts of the world, and for generation after generation they have worked a compulsive spell over travellers and naturalists alike.

The Hebrides are a world of rock and water, the half submerged edge of the continent where the sea has invaded the hills and valleys to form lochs and sounds, bays and inlets. Almost 550 islands, divided into two parallel archipelagoes called the Inner and Outer Hebrides, stretch for 240 miles along the western coast of Scotland. Some of these islands, like the inner Isle of Skye and the outer Isle of Lewis, are substantial in size. Others, like the Isle of Handa (one mile long, half a mile wide, 300 feet above sea level) or the remote islet of Sule Stack are mere pinpricks. Fewer than 70 of these islands are inhabited, some only by lighthouse keepers. With a total population of only 58,300 the

Hebrides remain one of the most deserted regions in Europe, and taking land surface only, there are fewer than 12 people per square mile—barely 5 per cent of the European average.

The landscape of the Hebrides is very worn and stark, the result of powerful erosion by the sea and Ice Age glaciers. The outer islands are largely composed of diamond-hard Lewisian gneiss well over 600 million years old. But some of the inner islands are made of much younger basalt, the remnants of volcanoes and vast beds of lava; in places this basalt has been eroded into extraordinary stacks or isolated columns of rock standing in the sea, or into towers and spires such as those of the Quiraing rock citadel and the Old Man of Storr on Skye. Elsewhere the basalt has solidified into curious hexagonal columns, such as those in Fingal's Cave on the tiny Isle of Staffa or the turreted northern face of Garbh Eilean on the Shiant Isles, where the columns are six feet in diameter.

For such northerly latitudes the climate is mild, owing to the ameliorating influence of the warm North Atlantic Drift or Gulf Stream, which gives the Hebridean seas an average surface temperature of 50°F. Snow is rare and rain, although frequent, is not as heavy as in the West Highlands where the mountains catch more than a hundred inches a year, one of the highest rainfalls in Europe. The dominating weather feature of the Hebrides is the wind; the prevailing south-westerlies are incessant and in winter can reach hurricane strength. To appreciate their full force, you have to go to the outlying islands, far-flung atoms of land like mountain tops towed out to sea: St. Kilda, North Rona, Sula Sgeir, Haskeir, the Flannans and the Monach Isles. At Barra Head in the Isles of Barra, small fish have been blown on to the top of the 630-foot cliff, and one great gale moved a 42-ton block of gneiss a distance of five feet. The Atlantic rollers crash against the cliffs of the outer isles with a massive impact that has been measured at three tons per square foot, constantly grinding away the rock.

The windward sides of these islands are fringed with dazzling white beaches of shell sand that stretch on, island after island, for a hundred miles and are lapped in fine weather by a sea of peacock hues. Behind the beaches lie sand dunes bound with marram grass; and beyond the dunes is a machair, or greensward, made highly fertile by the lime from the shell sand. In spring and summer the machair is covered with a carpet of wild flowers whose scent wafts out to ships at sea and flavours the milk of any cows that graze on them. If the great cliffs and sea stacks are the most awesome features of the Hebrides, the flower-strewn *machair* and bright shell-sand beaches are the most beautiful. By contrast, the leeward sides of the outer isles are covered with in-fertile peat bogs up to 20 feet deep, dotted with gnarled grey rocks and innumerable lochans of brown, acid water.

In the Hebrides, land and sea meet and react constantly. The islands, with their abundance of safe breeding sites on cliffs and stacks, provide homes for immense colonies of seabirds; while the Hebridean seas, which are rich in plankton, support vast numbers of fish—particularly mackerel and herring in shoals up to seven miles long—and so provide food for the birds. No other region in the world attracts so many different species of seabirds in such vast numbers; and few places can be so prodigal of marine life—from the giant squid, killer whale, dolphin and basking shark of the open sea, and the common seal and Atlantic grey seal in the great nurseries on North Rona, Haskeir and the Treshnish islands, to the humbler creatures of the pools and tidal zones, the acorn barnacles, the sand mason worms and hermit crabs.

Navigation among the islands is not an easy matter. The sea, with its tide rips, whirlpools, hidden reefs and sudden squalls, must be treated with extreme caution. But voyaging in these northern waters, in the orbit of seal bark and gannet cry, is something I can never forget.

For six months of one spring and summer I was a member of a project called Operation Seashore. Ten of us circumnavigated the entire 6,000-mile coastline of Britain in a 52-foot motor cruiser photographing and recording what we saw of the present state of the shore. The weather had been unkind at the start, and we advanced northwards along the east coast in blizzards and icy rain all through April and into May. Only when we had reached our most northerly position and passed through the much feared tide rips of the Pentland Firth—the so-called Merry Men of May where the North Sea meets the Atlantic Ocean—did the weather at last turn benign.

For a month we nosed along the north coast of Scotland and down through the Hebridean sea beyond Cape Wrath. For a month the sun beat down on us, daylight hardly ended, and we turned as brown as buccaneers. We had three tenders with us on our motor yacht—a small dinghy and two rubber inflatables; with these we periodically aban-doned our mother-ship and scurried off to explore the scatter of rocks and islands beyond our bow. Throughout the long hours of daylight we motored and rowed to hidden coves and rock-guarded islets looking for bird colonies or sea caves or whatever we could find.

On the inner Hebridean Isle of Skye a midday mist veils the Quiraing rocks, the weathered remains of basaltic lava from an ancient volcano.

If I close my eyes now, my head fills with remembered images of those island days, and I am again on the North Atlantic swell, the boat's bow butting the plankton-green sea, the gulls in our wake screaming above the bubbling of the outboard's exhaust. The frothy white line of the wake leads to a tiny bay and a beach of dazzling white sand; beyond it lies a flower-covered *machair* of milkwort and speedwell, and steep cliffs and a valley leading to an unknown interior. The sun is always shining in these memories, in spite of the northern latitude and the statistics for rainfall. Even reality had the quality of a dream; recalling it now I experience a pang of longing for that freedom.

I remember one scorching July day when I went off alone in an inflatable dinghy to a remote and tiny bay where probably no living soul had set foot for years. Access was possible only from the sea and I pointed the bow at the beach like an explorer arriving in an undiscovered land.

I throttled back the motor and the boat hissed up the sand. The beach was pristine—no footprint of man, no jetsam, no plastic bottles. I stepped ashore like Captain Cook or Vasco da Gama—for why should anyone have preceded me here, where there was no road, no tree, no spring? But as my naked foot left its first unmistakable imprint in the wet sand, I became aware that I was not alone. Two young stags stood out like unicorns at the head of the beach and watched my coming. They shied away at the sudden upturned white disc of my face, turned for a last brief stare, then moved slowly off. I followed after them, crushing the yellow and blue flowers of the *machair* underfoot, but they had mysteriously vanished among the rocks and bracken of the valley bottom. I was alone again. Silence. Then an echoing, peeling cry among the crags high above me, and another, and another—young bird voices, unformed, unsure, a loud anxious piping. Three bird shapes wheeled in tight circles close to a ledge on the cliff. They held their wings stiff, like glider's wings; and the configuration of the tips, broad and flared in silhouette against the sky, showed them to be buzzards. A larger adult bird launched itself off the ledge and joined the three gyrating juveniles, exhorting them with strident cries as they soared in larger and larger circles away from the security of the ledge, the comforts of the eyrie 300 feet up. They circled towards the head of the valley, then returned and soared above me.

It was hot. I looked back to the sea. My footprints marched up the beach towards me from the drawn-up boat. The receding sea was emerald green over the white sand bottom. Dark torpedo shapes nosed through the crystal water towards the weedless rocks—salmon, maybe,

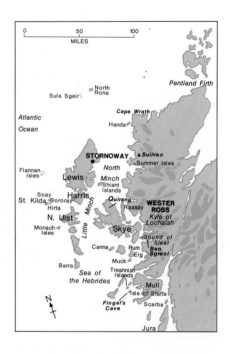

The Hebrides, or Western Isles, have one overriding justification for being called wild: they are remote, as the map indicates. Since the seas rose at the end of the Ice Age, they have been mere fragments of land strung out along the West Highland coast of Scotland, exposed to the Atlantic gales, divided by dangerous tide rips, and mostly uninhabited except by seabirds.

or sea trout. Rocks and islets, shimmering in the sun, appeared insubstantial, atomized. I took off my shirt and ran down the beach and leapt into the sea. The water closed over my head like a block of ice. Emerging, I cried out, like Robinson Crusoe, in order to hear my voice echo back to me—and as my shout rang between the basalt crags the buzzards fell silent and scurried through the air to the safety of their nest.

I remember other Hebridean images—images of natural prodigality and waste, curiously beautiful scenes of death and destruction on a scale that seemed somehow more appropriate to the tropics than these northern waters. I remember sleeping one night in the marram grass at the edge of a shell-sand beach on Skye and waking, sodden after a night of mist, to find a silver sea boiling with leaping mackerel and a school of bottle-nosed dolphins cruising up and down, feasting on the mackerel at their leisure.

I recall a time when the sea was so full of jellyfish I could not dip an oar in the water without hitting one; primitive organisms with brown or pink or purple nuclei, they pumped themselves through the ocean like transparent human hearts, oblivious of their own existence. For several weeks the jellyfish drifted by on the current that washed the islands; they entered the bays like a plague or were washed up on the beaches, where they lay, too insubstantial for even the gulls to scavenge, until they dissolved in the sun.

One still evening, when I was in the dinghy casting darrow lines for mackerel off the Isle of Canna, I had a visitor. Swimming slowly and making little more than one knot through the water, the visitor appeared from behind me and entered the extreme right-hand edge of my field of view, overhauling me barely an inch or two below the surface of the sea and no more than a foot from the side of the dinghy. The new arrival was the length of a London bus.

This was the first time I had ever seen a basking shark, the second biggest fish in the world (only the whale shark is bigger). The colossal grey-brown bulk and the weirdly silent, irresistibly buoyant passage of the creature barely an arm's length from me froze me to my seat. I hardly dared breathe or turn my head. Only my eyeballs moved; they watched the tip of the shark's nose slide forward above the surface, followed more than a boat's length later by the great, black, plastic-looking, triangular dorsal fin, standing a good two feet out of the water. The great fish slid forward, taking with it several fathoms of darrow lines, mere gossamer on such a vast and leathery back, until the tip of the flickering tail—describing arcs and parabolas and figures-of-eight like a skater on ice—drew level with where I sat.

It was the tail that I feared most. Simple mathematics told me that this giant fish, up to 35 feet long and weighing four and a half tons, could with a single lash of its seven-foot, half-ton tail easily capsize a boat a quarter of its length and a fraction of its weight. I was well aware that basking sharks are not carnivorous and graze only on plankton; I was equally aware that there have been almost no recorded incidents of basking sharks inflicting injury on man. But in the moment of sudden, unexpected close contact with great animals, reason deserts even the most hard-headed naturalist: confronted with that powerful tail, I could think only of the fate of open-boat whalers off Nantucket and of the blood-thirstiness of other kinds of sharks.

The shark's tail slid along the clinker-built hull of my dinghy with a delicate caress; then the tail flicked away and was drawn in the wake of the dorsal fin towards the near-by Isle of Muck. I turned my attention to my fishing lines; but I had hardly begun to disentangle them when I saw that the shark had changed direction and was approaching again, heading directly towards me. This time it passed down my port side and I had a clear view of the creature's vast mouth, held open to browse on a surface stratum of plankton. Staring into that spongy vortex, peering down that seemingly bottomless black throat, I experienced a curious twinge of vertigo, as Jonah must have done before he was drawn into the belly of the leviathan. Then, as the dorsal fin drew alongside, the shark dived. There was a slow stirring of its tapering afterquarters, a leisurely flick of the tail and the fin slid under the water like a submarine's conning tower. I peered down into the clear green ocean and watched my visitor sink soundlessly and recede into the gloom of the deep water. For a second or two its monstrous outline seemed to pulse on the farthest limit of visibility, and then it vanished in the darkness, leaving me alone on a long, oily Atlantic swell dotted with resting gulls.

On another occasion, I paid a visit to the Summer Isles off Wester Ross on the West Highland coast. With my companions from Operation Seashore I planned to photograph gull and tern nests on the islands, and in two inflatables we sallied forth along the craggy shore of Wester Ross across a sea as smooth and blue as lapis lazuli. Before long a small school of dolphins overtook us and leapt out of the sea on our starboard bow. Glistening streaks of streamlined muscle and fin, they hung in mid-air for the duration of an eye-blink, shedding showers of glittering water drops, before they were overtaken by gravity and shuddered

The branched casing or "tube" of a sand mason worm, composed of slime-bonded fragments of shell and sand, projects an inch or so above the sea floor in the shallow tidal zone of the Highland coast. Only the worm's pale green mouth is visible at the top of the tube; the rest of the creature lies protected within.

back into the waters of the North Minch. They found us slow, dull company. One of them surfaced beneath the inflatable in which I sat, its head pushing up the boat's thin rubber floor between my feet like a bank robber in a hooded mask. Then they were off after bigger entertainment —a seine-netter out of Stornoway, Lewis, on its way to herring grounds farther south. The dolphins shot away, arching through the sea with effortless power and grace, and left us silent in admiration and envy.

It stayed fine all that day and we spent most of it photographing Arctic terns' eggs hatching. It took half an hour or so of sporadic tapping and chipping for each fluffy brown chick to break out of its three-week entombment in a freckled shell and emerge into a world framed by four grinning men on their hands and knees, reeking of tobacco and two-stroke oil. Where the terns had built their colony, many herring gulls and skuas roamed the rocks foraging for unguarded chicks and eggs. It was easy to see they were up to no good; they shuffled nearer and nearer to their victim with ill-disguised voracity, eyes bright in cocked heads, beaks ready. Often the nesting terns rose up to drive them off. They swooped down on the aggressors like dive-bombers, their sharp bayonet bills to the fore. Sometimes, too, they dived down on the human intruders who squealed and ducked as the yellow beaks drilled into the top of their skulls. But some of the marauding gulls and skuas had grown indifferent to such attacks, which in fact inflicted no serious injury. These veterans were the real bandits. I watched them smash and drain an egg in a moment, or suddenly seize a newly hatched chick and, with a convulsive movement of the neck, swallow it whole in mid-flight. Sometimes the gulls were harried by their rival predators and forced to drop their prey; the helpless chick fell spinning down, but before it reached the surface of the sea it was caught by another gull or a skua and in a trice devoured alive.

Large numbers of birds were never far from us during our voyages of discovery. The gulls wheeled and screamed in our wake; the guillemots dived beneath our bows; whole tenements of seabirds would take off with an echoing clamour as we passed below the tall cliffs where they nested. It did not surprise us at all to learn that a large proportion of all the seabirds of the North Atlantic below the Arctic Circle breed on the islands of the Hebrides—24 species, in fact, including oceanic seabirds (gannet, fulmar, Manx shearwater, storm petrel, Leach's petrel, puffin, guillemot, razorbill), and coastal seabirds (gull, tern, cormorant, eider). Most of the world's population of gannets and Leach's petrels is

Coming in for a landing, a puffin displays three attributes that enable it to pursue fish underwater. Its narrow, stream-lined bill reduces water resistance; its large, webbed feet, used as rudders, help it to turn expertly; and its small, powerful wings beat rapidly like flippers beneath the waves to produce the speed for overtaking fish.

Anchored firmly to a rock, a plumose sea anemone, common along the Scottish coast, extends its delicate tentacles to feed (top and middle). The tentacles then spread and wave rhythmically in the water (bottom), sweeping floating food particles towards its central mouth.

contained on a few isolated rocks—justly famous sanctuaries like Ailsa Craig, Bass Rock, Handa, North Rona and St. Kilda.

As a species, seabirds are unusually long lived (some species may attain several score years) and spend a long time growing up. Much of a juvenile seabird's life is spent far out at sea, during which time it must learn to range over great distances, navigate accurately and live on the water, before returning home to breed. Many of the seabirds that breed in the Hebrides therefore spend a portion of their lives in very far-flung parts of the world indeed. The gannets pass years in distant nurseries off the Grand Banks of Newfoundland; the terns and skuas emigrate for a while to West Africa; the Manx shearwaters fly off to Argentina and have strayed as far as Australia; the Arctic skuas cross the world to the Antarctic pack ice. But in time they all return to the ledges and platforms and grass slopes and holes and cliffs of the summer breeding colonies of the British Isles.

The most exciting of these colonies and the most difficult of access are those of the outlying Hebridean islands, few of which have ever been settled. The exception is the most remote and most famous of all, St. Kilda, which for 2,000 years was inhabited by a curious community of Norse origin whose numbers dwindled until the last few survivors were evacuated at their own request in 1930. St. Kilda is the most spectacular island group in the Hebrides: four small islands of unbelievably tortured rock, containing the highest sea-cliffs in Britain (1,387 feet) and the highest stacks. To a biologist it is a treasure-house. It is home to three unique animals: the St. Kilda wren, the St. Kilda field mouse, and the mouflon-like Soay sheep, a relic of the domestic sheep of a millennium ago. In addition, there are 400,000 puffins, 90,000 and about 120,000 gannets—the largest gannet colony in the world.

Most of St. Kilda's gannets nest on a formidable, 1,245-foot-high islet called Bororay and two neighbouring sea-stacks. As you approach Bororay by boat from the main island of Hirta—not a matter to be taken lightly because of the heavy Atlantic swell that breaks without cease against the foot of the vertical rock wall—the noise of the birds becomes deafening. Gannets are not soft-spoken creatures; and when they are disturbed by the intrusion of man, they become screaming viragos, rattling and roaring without cease. *Urrah-rah-rah-rah-rah-rah-rah-rah* complains one gannet. *Urrah-rah-rah-rah-rah-rah-rah-rah* complain a hundred others. Wheeling past on six-foot wing spans, they darken the sky above you. The air is dizzy with swooping white bird shapes. Bird droppings hail down and discolour the sea round you; the

ANEMONE AT REST

TENTACLES EMERGING

FEEDING IN PROGRESS

cliffs are white with guano. Bobbing about in an open boat off the great stacks, it is easy to be overcome by the gannets' hectic brouhaha.

For me, in retrospect, the world of the Hebrides signifies gannets diving and shags in a cliff-face bird-slum, their wings stretched out stiff in the sun, reminding one of what they really are—warmed up reptiles with feathers. It is raven and buzzard locked beak and claw in angry embrace over Rum as they tumble together through several hundred feet of sky. It is Bororay, Canna, Eigg, Muck, Skye, Raasay, Scarba, Jura, Mull, Barra, Harris, North Uist and innumerable islands and islets I have barely glimpsed or whose names I do not know. It is the ever-changing colours of a skyscape rinsed clean by circling squalls and towering columns of rain, the aquamarine after-glow of the brief midsummer nights. It is the gunshot boom of the ocean swell exploding in the sea-caves; the clusters of yellow or red sea anemones in the rock pools; the brilliant, long beaches of white coral and crushed seashell, where the rocks are covered with the trailing white casts of the serpulid worm—indecipherable scrawls resembling Chinese ideograms—and where pink thrift burns brightly in the shallow clefts. I forget the days of discomfort and despair, when the air was saturated with salt spray, the world was obliterated by rain, and life seemed as sour and chill as the peat.

On the last day of the halcyon spell of anticyclonic calm during which we had navigated the Hebridean sea, I and the rest of the Operation Seashore crew cast off in our motor cruiser from Kyle of Lochalsh, negotiated the swirling 8 m.p.h. tide-race in the narrows of Kylerhea and entered the Sound of Sleat. The sky that day was of the purest royal blue—not a cloud, not a hint of rain, the barometer as steady as a rock, the air full of warm land smells of bog myrtle and young fern. A kind of festive spirit infected us that morning and we ran about the deck like South Sea islanders, heaving on ropes or throwing scraps to the following gulls.

As we advanced down the sound towards the open sea, the component parts of the seascape ahead began to resolve themselves into a once-familiar scene; it was as if I were entering the region of a half-forgotten dream. Dead ahead lay the Isle of Eigg, and craggy headlands sliding into the position in which I had remembered them. On the port bow lay a stubby, white lighthouse on a little island of rock and moss where wild sea otters used to have their holts. Perhaps they did still. I searched the sea through field glasses, but saw only the shearwaters scurrying low over the water, angling their wings to the crests and hollows of the waves as they followed the contours of the ocean.

We turned past the promontory of the farthest island and entered the bay. I recognized it, of course; I remembered every rock and tree of it. It was Camusfearna. Someone put out an anchor and it sank through the translucent water and threw up a puff of sand as it bit the bottom. We put an inflatable over the side and I climbed down into it with our Australian skipper. We motored to the beach without speaking. As I leapt ashore, the skipper said: "Nice little old spot."

"Yes," I replied, and added: "I've been here before, you know."

It was here that for one long winter I had held fort against the storms, with two otters for company and driftwood for fire. Now it was hot and still, yellow flag iris blazed in a patch of damp bog, bright orange lichen glowed on the grey rocks; the burn was almost dry after a month of drought, the waterfall only a whisper of its former torrential self. The place was more beautiful than I had remembered it, but it had changed beyond recall, and it was not the season that had changed it.

The house had gone, obliterated so completely that there was little indication it had ever existed. Not a brick or tile was left: just a square patch of fine rubble and sand on which the grass and nettles were already spreading. A fire had consumed the house one January night two years before, and the female otter, called Edal, had died in the blaze. My friend Gavin Maxwell had escaped unhurt from the flames and rescued the remaining otter, the male one called Teko, but everything else had been destroyed. Together they had started all over again in another deserted lighthouse cottage on a tiny island in the Narrows of Skye. But nothing had quite been the same again and within little more than a year Gavin was dead of cancer, outlived for no more than a week or two by the sole surviving otter.

I drew my foot through the rubble but no fragment of the past came back to me. A large block of granite dragged by Gavin's friends from the near-by cliffs marked the spot where his desk had once stood—the desk at which he had written his classic story of Camusfearna, *Ring of Bright Water*. Under the rowan tree near the burn was a small stone pile, surmounted by a plaque to commemorate the otter Edal. Some words by Gavin were inscribed on the plaque: "Whatever joy she gave to you give back to nature."

I crossed the burn and walked up the steep track along which I used to carry potatoes, fuel and other supplies, lurching into the wind on fitful black nights. It was still a hard climb up the first stretch and I paused to get my breath back at a kind of natural platform where the track bent sharply left. I looked back down. The boat rode quietly at anchor in the bay; sounds of laughter drifted up to me—a radio playing, a splash as someone dived off the stern. I turned to climb again and, as I did so, I caught sight of something curious and yet oddly familiar. In the very centre of a flat, grey rock lay a black animal dropping, still fresh in that hot sun. I looked at it and at once recognized the ground-up fish-bone texture. An otter had preceded me up this track. It must have scampered ahead of me only a few minutes before, paused at the same spot as I had and left this memento on the rock.

I was suddenly immensely glad. I called out in the silence, uttering my poor imitation of a range of otter cries, but no grey-brown shape came bounding through the bracken towards me, I saw no furry, round muzzle peering quizzically over the long grass, heard no chirruping response. I had hardly expected to. But I was grateful for that simple assurance, written boldly in a dropping on a rock, that confirmed the continuity of life at Camusfearna. Years before, the offspring of the wild sea otters in the bay had used the erstwhile cottage as a place where they could drop by for an egg or an eel on hunting trips away from home. And now, in spite of everything that had subsequently happened here, it was clear that otters still roamed the shores and hills of Camus-fearna, that in the end nothing had changed, the wilderness prevailed, only time had happened. It was an affirmation.

I turned back, and with a lighter heart retraced my steps towards the sea and the westering sun.

Seabirds and their Colonies

Carried by the relentless tide of instinct, millions of seabirds mass each spring to breed in colonies on the rocky coast of Scotland and its offshore islands. Petrels, gannets, auks, gulls and terns come in their flocks, and nesting sites that may have been visited for centuries again become centres of frantic activity.

The commotion in each colony intensifies as the birds select their mates, stake out their territories and then vigorously defend them. The raucous squabbling over nesting places rings out over the steep crags, drowning even the sound of the sea pounding against the rocks below.

In spite of their incessant clamour, the tenants of these avian tower-blocks manage to live and breed with a remarkable degree of order. Largely they do this by means of segregation, some species taking over whole cliffs for themselves, others occupying separate parts of the same cliff face. In addition, there is a code of behaviour among members of each species that prevents disputes erupting into bloodshed.

The tops of the cliffs are often chosen by roseate terns, although these birds also nest in coastal scrub. Both breeding sites are vulnerable to attack from larger, pira-tical gulls, and when such predators approach, the terns swarm nervously above their incubating mates.

Some of the highest ledges on the cliff faces are occupied by fulmars, large petrels that describe graceful parabolas in the air currents rising up over the cliffs (opposite). On ledges below the fulmars, pearly grey kittiwakes brood their young in crude nests of mud and grass or seaweed. Unlike many other gulls, which scavenge and sometimes even nest inland, the kittiwakes spend most of the year at sea, coming to land only at breeding time.

Often the kittiwakes' close neighbours are the guillemots, stumpy-winged, diving auks. Guillemots do not build nests, but simply deposit their eggs on inward sloping ledges where they are unlikely to be knocked inadvertently into the sea.

Perhaps the most spectacular of all the breeding colonies are those of the gannets. Since before the 10th Century they have flocked to rear their young on the remote islands of the St. Kilda group, arranging their nests to cover almost every inch of rock. About 45,000 breeding pairs have been recorded on the islands at one time—almost one quarter of the world's gannet population.

A FULMAR PREPARES TO LAND

GUILLEMOTS CROWD INTO THEIR CLIFF-LEDGE COLONY

KITTIWAKES AND A CORMORANT (TOP RIGHT) NESTING ON ROCKY TURRETS

ROSEATE TERNS AT THEIR BREEDING COLONY IN COASTAL SCRUB

GANNETS SWARMING ON A SEA STACK OFF ONE OF THE ST. KILDA ISLANDS

Bibliography

Atkinson, Robert, *Island Going.* Collins, 1949.

Bourlière, François, *The Land and Wild-Life of Eurasia.* Time-Life Books, 1973.

Brink, F. H. van der, *A Field Guide to the Mammals of Britain and Europe.* Collins, 1967.

Burton, Dr. Maurice, *Animals of Europe: The Ecology of the Wildlife.* Peter Lowe-Eurobook, 1973.

Chapman, Abel and Buck, Walter, *Wild Spain.* Gurney and Jackson, 1893.

Clark, Ronald W., *The Alps.* Weidenfeld and Nicolson, 1973.

Cleare, John, *Mountains.* Macmillan, 1975.

Corbet, G. B., *The Terrestrial Mammals of Western Europe.* Foulis, 1966.

Curry-Lindahl, Kai, *Europe: a Natural History.* Hamish Hamilton, 1964.

Darling, Sir Frank Fraser, *Naturalist on Rona.* Oxford University Press, 1939.

Darling, Sir Frank Fraser and Boyd, J. Morton, *The Highlands and Islands.* Collins, 1975.

Edlin, H. L., *Trees, Woods and Man.* Collins, 1956.

Egli, Emil and Müller, R. Hans, *Europe from the Air.* Harrap, 1959.

Ennion, E. A. R. and Tinberger, N., *Tracks.* Oxford University Press, 1967.

"European Bison, Current State of Knowledge and Need for Further Studies," in *Acta Theriologica,* Vol. 12, 1967. Proceedings of Second Symposium of the Mammal Section of the Polish Zoological Society, Bialowiecza, 1966.

Falynski, J. B. and Matuszkiewicz, W., *Der Urwald von Bialowiecza.* Warsaw-Bialowiecza, 1963.

Ferguson-Lees, James; Hockliffe, Quentin; Queeres, Ko, (Eds.), *A Guide to Bird-Watching in Europe.* The Bodley Head, 1975.

Fernández, Juan Antonio, *Doñana.* Editorial Olivo, 1974.

Fisher, James, Ed., "Woodlands" and "The Western Isles of Scotland" in *The New Naturalist: A Journal of British Natural History.* Collins, 1948.

Garms, Harry, *The Natural History of Europe.* Paul Hamlyn, 1967.

Gooders, John, *Where to Watch Birds in Europe.* Collins, 1975.

Graf, Jakob, *Animal Life of Europe.* Frederick Warne, 1968.

Hawkes, Jacquetta, *A Land.* Cresset Press, 1951.

Hoffman, George W., Ed., *A Geography of Europe.* Methuen, 1953.

Hoffman, Luc, *Camargue: the Soul of a Wilderness.* Harrap, 1971.

Houston, J. M., *The Western Mediterranean World: Introduction to its Regional Landscapes.* Longmans, 1964.

Körner, Albrecht and Vetter, Rainer R., *Wildnis der Wisente.* Leipzig, 1973.

Kümmerly, Walter, *The Forest.* Kümmerly and Frey, 1973.

Kurtén, Björn, *The Ice Age.* Hart-Davis, 1972.

L'Union Internationale pour la Conservation de la Nature et de ses Ressources, *Derniers Refuges: Atlas Commenté des Réserves Naturelles dans le Monde.* Elsevier, 1956.

Maclean, Charles, *Island on the Edge of the World.* Tom Stacey, 1973.

Marinatos, Spyridon, "Thera", in *National Geographic Magazine,* May 1972.

Marsh, George Perkins, *Man and Nature.* Sampson, Lowe and Searle, 1864.

Maxwell, Gavin, *Harpoon at a Venture.* Hart-Davis, 1952.

Maxwell, Gavin, *Ring of Bright Water.* Longmans, 1960.

Michener, James, *Iberia.* Corgi, 1971.

Mitchell, Alan, *A Field Guide to the Trees of Britain and Northern Europe.* Collins, 1974.

Mountfort, Guy, *Portrait of a Wilderness.* Hutchinson, 1968.

Murray, W. H., *The Islands of West Scotland, Inner and Outer Hebrides.* Eyre Methuen, 1973.

Naylor, John, *Andalusia.* Oxford University Press, 1975.

Noyce, Wilfrid, *Scholar Mountaineers.* Denis Dobson, 1950.

Okolow, C., "Zweifachen Jubiläum des Nationalparks von Bialowiecza", in *Die Sozialistische Forst Wirtschaft.* East Berlin, 1975.

Peterson, Roger, Mountfort, Guy and Hollon, P. A. D., *A Field Guide to the Birds of Britain and Europe.* Collins, 1974.

Piggot, Stewart, *Ancient Europe: a Survey.* Edinburgh University Press, 1967.

Polunin, Oleg, *The Concise Flowers of Europe.* Oxford University Press, 1974.

Pop, Emil and Salagenu, N., *Nature Reserves in Romania.* Bucharest, 1975.

Saunders, David, *Seabirds.* Hamlyn, 1971.

Stenuit, Robert, *Caves.* Nicholas Vane, 1966.

Steel, Tom, *The Life and Death of St. Kilda.* National Trust for Scotland, 1965.

Talpeanu, M. and Paspaleva, M., *Oiseaux du Delta du Danube.* Bucharest, 1973.

Tyndale, John, *The Glaciers of the Alps.* J. M. Dent, 1906.

Ucko, Peter J. and Dimbleby, G. W., *The Domestication and Exploitation of Plants and Animals.* Duckworth, 1969.

Vial, A. E. Lockington, *Alpine Glaciers.* Blatchworth Press, 1952.

Williamson, Kenneth and Boyd, J. Morton, *St. Kilda Summer.* Hutchinson, 1960.

Zabinski, Jan and Krysiak, Kazimierz, *The European Bison.* State Council for the Conservation of Nature, Poland, 1960.

Acknowledgements

Janet Barber, World Wildlife Fund, Godalming; Terenia Bartel, London; Louise Botting, London; J. K. Burras, Oxford; Giles Camplin, Farnham, Surrey; Dr. Javier Castroviejo, Estación Biológica de Coto Doñana, Spain; Professor J. Cloudesley-Thompson, London; Charles Dettmer, Thames Ditton, Surrey; Fred Dolder, Zurich; Brian Featherstone and Martine Cazan, Simiane La Rotonde, Provence; Dr. Peter Francis, Open University, Milton Keynes, Buckinghamshire; Dr. Ion Fuhn, Bucharest; Dr. David George, British Museum (Natural History), London; Director and staff of the Gran Paradiso National Park, Italy; Alice Grandison, British Museum (Natural History), London; Sally Heathcote, British Museum (Natural History), London; Christopher Hill, British Museum (Natural History), London; Dr. J. Jewell, British Museum (Natural History), London; Kurt and Diana Klein, Geneva; Mgr. Inz. Stefan Krukowski, Bialowieza National Park, Poland; Dr. J. Morton Boyd, Nature Conservancy for Scotland, Edinburgh; Calum M. Munro, Highlands and Islands Development Board, Inverness; Dr. Czeslaw Okolow, Bialowieza National Park, Poland; Cladiade Paniote, Sf. Gheorghe Nature Reserve, România; Roger Perry, Bradfield St. George, Suffolk; Wleodzimierz Piroznikow, Bialowieza National Park, Poland; Anthony Smith, London; John Thackray, British Museum (Geology), London; Dr. John Thornes, London School of Economics; Professor J. A. Valverde, Seville; Director and staff of Vanoise National Park, Savoy; Bud Young, Dept. of Overseas Development, London.

Picture Credits

Cover–Douglas Botting. Front end papers 1, 2–Gerhard Klammet. Front end paper 3, page 1–Brian Hawkes from Natural History Photographic Agency, Westerham, Kent. 2, 3–John Cleare/Mountain Camera. 4, 5–René Pierre Bille. 6, 7–J. S. Wightman from Ardea, London. 8, 9–N. A. Callow from Natural History Photographic Agency. 14, 15–Map by Hunting Surveys Ltd., London. 20–Douglas Botting. 23–John Cleare/Mountain Camera. 27–Aldo Durazzi. 29–N. A. Callow from Natural History Photographic Agency. 30–Werner Curth from Ardea. 35–Walter Fendrich. 36, 37–Werner Zepf. 38, 39–Chris Mylne from Ardea. 40–Werner Zepf. 41–Neville Fox Davies from Bruce Coleman Ltd., London. 42, 43–Werner Zepf. 47–Chris Bonington from Bruce Coleman Ltd. 49–Map by Hunting Surveys Ltd. 51–Christopher Grey-Wilson. 58, 59–Mansell Collection, London. 60–J. P. Ferrero from Ardea. 65–Christopher Grey-Wilson. 66–A. J. Sutcliffe from Natural Science Photos, London. 71–Hans Rheinhard from Bruce Coleman Ltd. 73–Ake Lindau from Ardea. 74, 75–De Biasi from Mondadori Press. 76–Claude Pissavini from Jacana, Paris. 79–Fred Winner from Jacana. 70 to 78–Wood engravings from Historiae Animalium by Conrad Gesner, 1551-1587, by courtesy of The Trustees of the British Museum (Natural History), London. 82–J. F. Preedy from Tony Stone Associates Ltd., London. 86–Douglas Botting. 91–Charles Mikolaycak. 93–Douglas Botting. 97–M. W. F. Tweedie from Natural History Photographic Agency. 98–D. M. T. Ettlinger from Natural Science Photos. 99 to 101–J. L. Mason from Ardea. 102, 103–Jane Burton from Bruce Coleman Ltd. 106–I. R. Beames from Ardea. 109–Douglas Botting. 110–Map by Hunting Surveys Ltd. 112–P. A. Bowman from Natural Science Photos. 113–M. Chinery from Natural Science Photos. 114–Brian Hawkes from Natural History Photographic Agency. 116–Juan A. Fernandez from Bruce Coleman Ltd. 117–F. Ontañon from Safoto, Madrid. 121–Leo Dickinson. 122, 123–N. A. Callow from Natural History Photographic Agency. 124–Anthony Howarth from Susan Griggs Agency, London. 125–Su Gooders from Ardea. 126, 127–Walter Fendrich. 128, 129–Gerhard Klammet. 132–John G. Walmsley. 135–Antonio Camoyan Perez. 136–Litia Fernandez from Bruce Coleman Ltd. 141–Antonio Camoyan Perez. 144 to 154–Douglas Botting. 155–John Burton. 159–C. M. Dixon. 160–Map by Hunting Surveys Ltd. 163–Les Jackman from Natural History Photographic Agency. 165–David and Katie Urry from Bruce Coleman Ltd. 166–Heather Angel from Biophotos. 171–B. L. Sage from Ardea. 172, 173–A. Butler from Natural History Photographic Agency. 174, 175–Brian Hawkes from Natural History Photographic Agency. 176, 177–Leslie Brown from Ardea. 178, 179–Tom Weir.

Index

Numerals in italics indicate a photograph or drawing of the subject mentioned.

Colour reproduction by Irwin Photography Ltd., at their Leeds PDI Scanner Studio.
Filmsetting by C. E. Dawkins (Typesetters) Ltd., London, SE1 1UN
Printed and bound in Belgium by Brepols Fabrieken N.V.

XXXX